LEAD
LIKE A
CEO

THE 90 DAY
LEADERSHIP OPERATING SYSTEM
TO LEAD BOLDLY, BUILD STRATEGICALLY
AND SCALE YOUR IMPACT

JIM SALIBA

Prominence Publishing

www.prominencepublishing.com

Lead Like a CEO / Jim Saliba -- 1st ed.

ISBN: 978-1-997649-07-6

"Leadership isn't about the title.
It's about acting like you own the place."

What People Are Saying

"I couldn't put it down once I started. This book doesn't waste any time: Get ready for the tough talk no one else is giving you, backed up with a realistic plan and changes you can make immediately to transform your leadership."

— Leslie Hoffman, Sr. Director of Creative – Emerging Brands;
Kendo Brands

* * *

"In **Lead Like a CEO**, Jim Saliba pulls no punches in confronting the messy realities of leadership, whether they be our fears, daily emergencies, entrenched organizational cultures, or other barriers he addresses. With a structure that encourages self-reflection, practical exercises, and iterative learning, the book empowers leaders to take ownership of their growth and lead more confident, effective teams."

– Albert Faro, MD, Senior Vice President & Chief Medical Officer –
Cystic Fibrosis Foundation

* * *

"**Lead Like a CEO** provides clear, relatable tactics and perspectives that are immediately actionable through a lens of experience not thought."

— Matthew Batey, COO – Teatro Group

"Jim has a remarkable gift for transforming the most challenging and impactful role of being a CEO into something deeply relevant and personal. He helps you not just lead, but envision—guiding you to shape a mission that leaves a lasting, positive mark on the world. This book is an essential tool every CEO should keep in their toolbox."

— *Jagruti B. VP of Business Development*

* * *

"James Saliba uses **Lead like a CEO** to surgically address how to show up and define your path and role to being a CEO of your own space. It taught me to design my role to what is actually needed."

— *James Watson VP of Support Smartsheet*

Dedication

To the ones who keep showing up,
even when it's messy, uncertain, or thankless.
The leaders who carry the weight no one sees,
make the call no one wants to make,
and still believe there's a better way to lead.
You are the reason this book exists.

To my clients:
Thank you for letting me into your real moments,
not just the polished ones.
You've taught me what courage actually looks like
in a boardroom, a Zoom room, and a 10 p.m. Slack message.
You are building something that matters.

To my family:
To Dolores and Michelle, watching you lead your own lives
has been the most humbling and beautiful lesson
in presence, resilience, and grace.
To Antoinette, thank you for being the steady
rhythm behind every wild idea.
You've given me the space to chase my voice,
and the roots to come back home to it.
This book is for the builders, the truth-tellers,
and the ones still learning as they lead.

Get Your Bonus Tools + Leadership Downloads

Want the full set of tools, worksheets, and experiment templates that go with this book?

We've created a **free bonus resource kit** to help you:

- Run your own leadership experiments

- Design your 90-Day Ascent Plan

- Audit your systems, culture, and leadership habits

- Track momentum with flywheels, scoreboards, and R/Y/G scans

You'll get:

- 15 downloadable worksheets (one per chapter)

- Bonus Toolkit: Design Better Experiments with AI

- The "Own Your Area" self-assessment

No filler. Just tools that work.

Grab everything here: https://jamessaliba.com/leadlikeaceobonus

Contents

Preface

If you've read my earlier books, you'll notice something different right away. I wrote those as James Saliba. This one? It's from Jim. Because this book isn't just a framework. It's me, in real time, talking to you the way I talk to every leader I coach.

Why This Book Exists

You don't need a title to lead. You don't need permission to build. You need a system that actually works. One you can run with clarity, confidence, and guts. That's what this book gives you. A repeatable 90-day operating system to lead, build, and scale your impact from wherever you sit.

This isn't a manual for climbing the ladder or playing it safe. *Lead Like a CEO* was built for leaders who are ready to claim their space now, without waiting for someone else to hand it to them. It's for those ready to lead *right now*, not because someone handed them a title, but because they've decided to take ownership where they are.

You don't need a bigger office to lead like a CEO. You need a better mindset and a better playbook.

That's what this book is.

My Story

After decades in tech, from engineer to executive, and later consulting on large transformations, I kept seeing the same patterns.

Leaders weren't stopping to look around. They weren't stepping back to read the signs, understand their strengths and gaps, and intentionally steer their area forward. That's what led me to write **Reviving the Work Environment.** (OMG, what a terrible title, but a decent idea)

It helped leaders pause, assess, and confront the gap between where they are and where they need to lead next. To take a simple but vital first step: **understand yourself, understand your environment, visualize, and act.**

But it didn't go far enough. Awareness was just the beginning. I saw the need for a better system, a way to build a plan, create momentum, and move with clarity. That's why I wrote **The Six-Step Leadership Challenge.**

It offered leaders a practical framework:

- Understand the system.

- Choose strategic moves.

- Build a deliberate plan to grow, lead, and repeat.

It gave leaders **better tools. Better frameworks. Better steps.** And still, it wasn't enough. Because tools, frameworks, and even great ideas only get you so far.

You know the drill. You pick up a book, and it drops a single concept or framework in your lap, then calls it a day. It sounds good, but it doesn't help you turn it into daily moves that actually change how you lead.

That's where people get stuck.

That's where companies stall.

That's where potential goes to waste.

A few years ago, I caught a documentary about the history of Lego, and something clicked. In the early days, Lego was just a brick company. Brilliant, flexible, open-ended little blocks. They sold the parts, but not the picture. And it worked… for a while.

But eventually, sales plummeted. At one point, they were losing nearly a million dollars a day. Distribution was scattered. In the U.S., they were sold through Samsonite. The business was drifting, directionless. Kids loved the concept, but they didn't always know what to build with it.

Then Lego changed the game.

They stopped just selling *pieces* and started selling *projects*. Complete kits with a vision, a goal, instructions, and exactly what you needed to build something that felt epic.

And suddenly, it wasn't just a toy anymore; it was an engine of creativity, momentum, and clarity. Lego became the powerhouse they are today, not just because of the brick, but because they gave people a **system** for building something real.

Leadership is no different.

I see it all the time: lots of disconnected bricks, ideas, tools, theories, but no system to build something real. But without a mission, a structure, or a rhythm? That pile of bricks doesn't build anything.

You need a **project kit**. A clear mission. The right tools assembled the right way. The system, the mindset, and the motion to build something bigger.

Lead Like a CEO is your leadership project kit. It pulls together everything you need to think differently, act strategically, and lead your space like a CEO, no permission slips required.

What You'll Get Here

This book is a **90-day playbook** for stepping up, tightening your systems, and leading at the level you're capable of, whether your job title catches up to you or not.

You'll learn how to:

- Build a bold vision and start acting on it immediately.

- Tighten your systems and focus where it truly matters.

- Amplify your leadership brand and create real durability in your results.

- Drive execution with purpose and create a leadership rhythm that lasts.

This isn't about *knowing* more. It's about **building** more, and doing it deliberately, fast, and visibly.

A Note Before You Dive In

This isn't a book you skim. It's a book you *run*.

Each section challenges you to experiment, reflect, and lead more boldly. Treat it like a leadership laboratory, a place to test, adapt, and grow. If you do, you won't just become more strategic. You'll start to **Lead Like a CEO**, building results, trust, and visibility that can't be ignored.

Leadership isn't a title. It's a decision.

Make it.

Let's go!

Introduction: Start Where You Are

Leadership isn't about the title.
It starts the moment you say, "This is mine."

– Jim Saliba

Let me guess, you've got the title, the workload, the pressure… and you're still waiting for permission to lead.

You've earned the role. Or at least, you've earned enough trust to be responsible for people, projects, deliverables, revenue, reputation, or maybe all of it at once. But somewhere between the all-hands meetings, the back-to-back calendars, and the thousand tiny decisions you're forced to make every week, you're starting to wonder: *Is this leadership? Or just a slow, sweaty descent into glorified middle management?*

Because here's what you won't find in the job description: **Leadership isn't about the title. It starts the moment you say, "This is mine."**

You won't find recycled advice here. What you'll get is a system for turning your experience into momentum so you can lead visibly, strategically, and on purpose. It's for leaders who are done waiting and ready to act like they own the place. Because if you don't claim your space, someone else will. If you're looking for a book to pat you on the back and tell you that your burnout is just a phase and your boss will eventually notice how hard you're working, close this book now. Seriously. Go do some meditation and come back when you're ready for the truth.

Because this book? This book is a push. It's not soft. It's not fluffy. It won't tell you to wait your turn. This is a book about stepping up, stepping forward, and stepping into leading like a CEO, whether or not anyone has handed you the keys to the corner office.

Why This Book

Because I'm tired of watching great people shrink themselves while mediocre leadership floats up. Because I'm tired of seeing brilliant directors get stuck acting like project managers, and VPs acting like team leads. Because I've coached enough leaders at every level to know that most of the time, the problem isn't them.

It's the system.

A system that rewards technical excellence, then punishes you for not being instantly brilliant at managing people. A system that says, "Be strategic," but drowns you in status reports. A system that treats leadership like a perk you get after you've put in your dues, instead of a mindset you choose to build every damn day.

Coach's Commentary

If this sounds familiar, good. You're not crazy. The system's just broken, and we're here to build you a better one.

Leadership doesn't come after promotion. It doesn't come after training. It comes after you decide to lead.

And let me get on a little soapbox here. I read a stat a while back that stuck with me: Formal leadership training often comes ten years *after* someone's already in the role. Ten. Years. What the hell were they doing for those ten years? Babysitting? Managing chaos? Faking it while hoping no one noticed? And then, finally, someone hands them a shiny binder after a two-day offsite leadership workshop and says, "Now you're trained."

No wonder people are burned out.

Training that sits in a drawer, or buried in your Kindle, doesn't build leadership. Promotions don't magically change how you show up. You know what does? Taking responsibility for your space before anyone else volunteers you for it. Deciding that you're not going to wait for clarity, you're going to create it.

And the higher you go, the weirder it gets, because here's what I hear from the C-suite: "My leadership team is filled with glorified managers. They're competent, but they're still asking for permission. They still wait for me to make the call."

So, what does that make the C-Suite executive? The babysitter of glorified, capable-but-needy managers who are still waiting to be told what to do?

No, thanks.

I wrote this book to hand you the tools I wish someone had given me. The mental models, the experiments, the reframes, and the permission slip to lead the way you were always meant to.

Why Now

Because the world has changed, and fast. In just the past five years, we've had a global pandemic that redefined where and how we work. We've seen the rise of distributed teams spanning time zones from San Francisco to Shanghai. Companies now operate on a 24/7 cycle with people collaborating from California to Poland to Hyderabad. And if you blinked, you may have missed the part where AI went from background buzz to center stage.

A month ago, I walked into one of those airport magazine shops, just looking to grab something to read on a flight. One magazine headline practically screamed off the rack: "AI: The Fastest Moving Technology Mankind Has Ever Seen."

And they're not wrong.

What we're living through right now isn't a tech trend. It's a tidal wave. It's not just reshaping jobs; it's reshaping expectations. Decision-making is faster. Strategy cycles are shorter. And the pressure to be more visible, more valuable, and more visionary has never been higher.

So, if you're still stuck waiting for someone to give you permission and drowning in meetings, firefighting, and second-guessing your worth while trying not to sound too bold or too vulnerable…

That's not going to cut it anymore.

This isn't the moment to stay quiet or play it safe. This is the moment to step up, get clear, and start leading with intent, because the future is already moving, and your leadership needs to move with it.

Why Me

I started in tech. A programmer. A systems guy. The one who knew how things connected and how to make them move. Over time, I climbed. Manager. Director. VP. Eventually, I led nearly 200 people at a multi-billion-dollar software company. I was responsible for products, processes, and people that directly impacted the bottom line. On paper? I looked like a seasoned executive. Inside? I was still winging it, faking it till I made it.

No one tells you how to lead. They just give you a team and say, "Go."

So I did what most high performers do: I worked harder. I fixed everyone's problems. I stayed late. I micromanaged. I thought being indispensable would make me irreplaceable. Apparently, exhaustion is not a promotion strategy. It only made me exhausted.

Then I met Rob.

Rob was my new GM. I hadn't even made it to our first one-on-one before I started sweating, because he'd already let a few of my peers go.

He walks in, drops into the chair across from me, and says, "There's a team in my Brand Unit that doesn't know how to release a product, no matter how long I give them. I want you to take their process, burn it down to the nap, and rebuild it."

So, I asked a question. Something basic. And he hit me with: "I don't know. That's what the fuck I have you for."

That line changed everything. Rob didn't want updates. He wanted outcomes. He expected me to lead. From that day forward, I stopped sending approval-seeking emails and started writing: "Here's the issue. Here's the solution. I'm moving forward unless I hear otherwise in 24 hours."

Rob never responded, except once. Even then, it was just a quick note: "Hold up on this one till we talk. I've got more context." That was it. That was the moment I stopped waiting for permission, and that's what I want for you.

I come from tech, and I still coach deep inside it. Today, I work with senior leaders across Amazon, PayPal, Capital One, global health systems, disease foundations, financial institutions, and fast-scaling startups. Directors, VPs, CTOs, CMOs, COOs, even CEOs. Most are U.S.-based, but many are global. Some are new to the role, while others are hitting the hardest stretch of their career. But every one of them reaches the same point where the old playbook fails, and a deeper kind of leadership has to kick in.

The stories in this book are drawn from those experiences. They're composite. I've blended client moments, coaching breakthroughs, and real-world experiments to help you find yourself in them. This isn't theory. This is how the work *actually* gets done.

You're not here to lead by someone else's blueprint. You're here to build the one that fits your story, your strengths, and your climb.

A Story: Sarah's Invisible CEO Moment

Sarah was a Senior Manager of Strategy and Growth at a fast-moving finance and consulting firm. She wasn't just a strong performer; she was the glue. When things broke, Sarah fixed them. When people slipped, Sarah caught them. She held the team together, quietly, powerfully, and almost invisibly.

The real problem? She didn't see herself as a leader yet. She still thought of herself as "the helper." And so did everyone else.

Coach's Commentary

Still calling yourself "just the helper?" You're not. If the team collapses without you, it's time to step forward, not shrink back.

When we sat down for coaching, I asked, "What would happen if you stopped doing all of this?"

She paused. Blinked. "Honestly, the team would fall apart."

"Exactly," I said. "So, let's stop calling you the support person and start calling you what you are, the CEO of this space."

And she did. She started naming her leadership. Acting with authority. Making decisions without apology. And you know what happened? Everyone else adjusted their lens, too. She didn't just claim her space; she made others recognize it, and that's the shift this book is here to help you make.

A Story: David's Wake-Up Call

David Chen had the title. He had the responsibility. He had the team. In fact, he'd just been promoted to Chief Technology Officer after years of scaling fast-growth SaaS companies, and now he found himself juggling two jobs. He hadn't backfilled his old engineering role, so while trying to act like a CTO, he was still stuck deep in the weeds, dragging his past job along behind him like a heavy duffel bag. He rolled out new architecture plans. Defined platform strategies. Reorganized pods. It looked great on paper, but something was missing. Something important.

One day, during one of our coaching sessions, we were circling a familiar loop, tech debt mounting, product teams stalled, decisions bottlenecked at his desk. He got quiet. Thought for a minute. Then he said, "I'm starting to realize something. I've been trying to lead by designing processes. But I haven't actually stepped into the seat. I'm still carrying the water for the last CTO. I haven't made this mine yet."

That moment? That was the leadership snap. David realized that owning the seat wasn't about optimizing systems or managing execution. It was about raising the strategic altitude. Leading from a new place, with a new mandate.

From that day on, he started showing up differently, reframing every decision based on where the company needed to go next, not just what it needed to manage today. His language evolved, his energy changed, his peers felt it, and his cross-functional partners noticed.

You don't need to start from scratch. But you do need to decide that this is yours now, because once you say, "I own this," you stop being the caretaker of yesterday's code and start becoming the architect of tomorrow's success.

That's what this chapter is about. That's what this book is here for.

What This Book Is (and Isn't)

This isn't about theory. And it's not feel-good filler either. This is not about waiting for your next role. This is a practical, unapologetic, 90-day playbook for owning your space, building your story, and leading like a CEO.

And let me be clear: I've read the books. Hundreds of them. I have over 400 leadership and business books in my library, not even counting the ones I've listened to on Audible while pacing airport terminals or driving to client sessions. I constantly hunt for material to support the leaders I coach. Some of those books are excellent. But most? Flat. Two-dimensional. Focused on one sliver of what leadership means.

Books on coaching. Books on emotional intelligence. Books on time management. Books on strategy. Books on systems. Books on culture. All important, but siloed. They give you a tool, maybe two, but they don't give you the system for how all of it fits together.

This book is different.

This book is about integration. It's about creating a system that holds all the pieces you've collected and helps you *actually use them* to lead.

It's not a miracle book on how to coach. It's not the definitive word on how to delegate. It's not a crash course on how to build psychological safety in your team. It's the playbook for how to take all of that, plus your lived experience, and plug it into a rhythm of leadership growth.

Because great leaders don't stand still. They don't assume what worked last year will work next year. They don't assume what worked in their last company will work in this one. Experience matters, but it's not the full story.

You need a way to test, adapt, and grow.

This book is for people who already know they're capable of more, even if no one has handed them the title yet. It's for leaders who are done waiting and ready to act like they own the place. Because if you don't claim your space, someone else will.

That's what my Six-Step Leadership Challenge and the L.E.A.D. Lab are built for.

You'll learn:

- The Six-Step Leadership Challenge (Introspection, Extrospection, Storyboard Your Future, Action Strategy, Action + Reaction, Retrospect + Celebrate)

- The L.E.A.D. Lab (Lean into, Empower, Amplify, and build Durability for your story)

- How to create clarity, direction, and momentum in 90-day cycles

You'll walk through stories, tools, and coaching experiments that turn insight into practice, and you'll stop wondering if you're leading and start seeing the evidence of it every week.

What It Means to Lead Like a CEO

Leading like a CEO isn't about hierarchy. It's not about a promotion. It's not about waiting for someone to hand you a bigger title. It's about taking full ownership, right now, of everything you touch, shape, lead, and influence. It means:

- Seeing your role not as a set of tasks, but as a business you are responsible for growing.

- Thinking like an owner, not a renter. Protecting the mission, the culture, the systems, because they're *yours* to build, not just manage.

- Making bold moves based on the bigger picture, not just reacting to whatever fire is burning hottest today.

- Creating value beyond your job description. Driving outcomes, not just outputs. Building momentum that lasts longer than your own effort.

- Leading like you're the only one responsible for the future health, growth, and culture of your domain, because you are.

When you lead like a CEO, you stop waiting for permission. You stop asking for clarity, you create it. You stop working to get noticed, you work to create undeniable value. And when you do that, the titles, the recognition, the career acceleration? They stop being the goal and start becoming the byproduct.

Because no one hands you ownership. You earn it in ways people can't dismiss.

Coach's Commentary

Your career doesn't change because you hope someone notices you. It changes when you start leading like they can't afford not to

About the Stories in This Book

Every story you'll read in this book is based on real client conversations. The names, roles, and companies have been changed to protect privacy, but the challenges, turning points, and victories are all rooted in the messy, brilliant reality of the leaders I've coached over the years.

Nearly all of the stories, Sarah, Michael, David, Tonya, are composites, blended from multiple clients facing similar struggles. They represent the patterns I see again and again across industries, functions, and leadership levels.

You may see a bit of yourself in Sarah, or Michael, or someone else you meet along the way. That's by design. These stories aren't meant to be perfect; they're meant to be true, relatable, and useful, because if you recognize yourself in their stuckness, you'll also recognize yourself in their growth.

And maybe, just maybe, you'll stop asking, "Could this be me?" and start saying, "This *is* me."

How This Book Works

This isn't a sit-back-and-nod book. It's a **90-day leadership laboratory** you run while you move. Each chapter is built to shift you fast, from thought to action to visible results. The rhythm is deliberate:

Big Reality Check

We open fast, by hammering a myth, breaking a leadership illusion, or calling out the traps most books dance around, because **clarity beats comfort. Always.**

Story to Wake You Up

Not case studies. Not theory. Real leaders, real struggles, real turning points, because movement beats memorization.

Reframe to Shift Your Lens

You can't lead differently if you still see leadership the way you always have. We sharpen your vision first, then your execution.

Tools and Experiments to Drive Action

Every chapter arms you with **leadership experiments** you can run inside your next 90-Day Ascent Loop. You'll see more experiments packed into Chapters 7–10 as you design your next moves.

Driving Question + Jim's Coaching Question

Each chapter hands you two key jolts:

1. **The Driving Question** forces you to wrestle with a new leadership lens.

2. **Jim's Coaching Question** pushes you to get personal, tactical, and brutally honest with yourself.

Answer both? You don't just think differently, you start *leading differently.*

Mini Challenge

Every chapter hands you one small, immediate action you can run now, not later. Momentum doesn't come from big plans. It comes from small, sharp moves stacked fast.

Final Reframe

Each chapter ends with one unforgettable anchor, an idea meant to stay with you long after you put the book down.

You've probably noticed the short 'Coach's Commentary' lines. We continue these throughout the book. They're quick, sticky takeaways designed to travel with you and show up when you need them most. They're what I'd whisper in your ear right before a big meeting, or what I'd text you if you needed a leadership jolt mid-week: simple, memorable, and sharp enough to shift your mindset in one sentence.

Coach's Commentary

Don't just read this, run it. Leadership is a contact sport. You'll learn faster by moving than by mulling

How This Book Aligns With The Six-Step Leadership Challenge

If you've read my last book, *The Six-Step Leadership Challenge*, you already know the system:

Step 1: Introspection
Step 2: Extrospection
Step 3: Storyboard Your Future
Step 4: Action Strategy
Step 5: Action + Reaction
Step 6: Retrospect + Celebrate

That framework gives you the structure. **This book gives you the real-world playbook.**

Here's how *Lead Like a CEO* builds on it:

Six-Step Leadership Challenge Step	Chapters in This Book	Focus
Step 1: Introspection	1–2	Knowing yourself, your story, your strengths, and your leadership patterns.
Step 2: Extrospection	3–4	Understanding the system you're leading inside, the culture, and the unspoken rules.
Step 3: Storyboard Your Future	5–6	Crafting a bold, living vision for what you're building.
Step 4: Action Strategy	7–10	Building your 90-Day Ascent Plan through the L.E.A.D. Lab (Lean, Empower, Amplify, Durability).
Step 5: Action + Reaction	11–12	Running the first 30-Day Flywheel, adjusting in real-time, and learning while moving.
Step 6: Retrospect + Celebrate	13–14	Closing the full 90-Day Ascent Loop, harvesting lessons, and locking in momentum.

The final two chapters (15 and 16) go even further:

- Helping you **architect your next 90-Day Ascent** even smarter.

- Owning the leadership story you're building now, by design, not default.

This book doesn't just revisit the Six Steps. It **runs** them, with a clear, actionable rhythm built for leaders who are ready to move, not just study.

Where *The Six-Step Leadership Challenge* gave you the tools, *Lead Like a CEO* hands you the project kit, the flywheels, ascent loops, experiments, and feedback rhythms, that will make leadership visible, scalable, and inevitable.

Try It Now: Mini Challenge

Before we get into Chapter 1, let's get tactical:

Create your first Own Your Area Map.

Write down everything you currently own, shape, lead, or influence. People, systems, outcomes, relationships, decisions. Don't edit it. Don't overthink it. Just name what's yours, because leadership starts with clarity, and clarity starts here.

🖊 Download Worksheet: W0 – Own Your Area Map Worksheet

Final Reframe: You Don't Need Permission

You don't need a new title to lead like a CEO. You don't need a strategy deck blessed by three committees. And you definitely don't need to wait for someone in a higher-up box on the org chart to say you're ready. You need a plan. You need a rhythm. You need a shift, from waiting to acting, from reacting to owning.

The work of leadership starts not with permission, but with ownership. It begins the moment you say: "This is mine."

If you remember nothing else, remember this:

Leadership doesn't start with permission. It starts when you decide to own it.

That moment? It starts now. And in the next chapter, we're going to map it. We'll name what you already own, what you touch, shape, and influence, so you can stop playing small in your own domain and start leading it with clarity.

You're not just learning leadership. You're engineering it, one flywheel at a time.

CHAPTER 1

You're Already the CEO.
You Just Haven't Claimed It Yet

Leadership doesn't start when you get the title.
It starts when you own what's already true.

– Jim Saliba

You're Already in Motion, But Are You Actually Leading?

You're already in charge of something. Maybe your title still says "Manager," "Director," or "Team Lead." Maybe you've made it to VP or even the C-suite. Maybe you're technically "acting" in the role. Doesn't matter. People are already moving around you. They send things your way before taking action. They loop you in for decisions. They wait for your nod. You're not just showing up, you're steering more than you realize.

This isn't about chasing the next promotion. It's about recognizing that you've already stepped into leadership, maybe without meaning to. You don't wake up one morning magically feeling ready. You wake up realizing people are already depending on you. And in that space between being counted on and truly owning the role, a lot of opportunity slips through, because if you don't claim what you're already leading, you'll keep operating one or two levels below where you belong. You'll keep softening your ideas, second-guessing your authority, and overcompensating with busyness instead of intention.

Leadership doesn't start with a title. It starts with a shift, from being responsible *for* something, to being responsible *to* **it.**

David's Shift From Carrying to Leading

David Chen didn't have a leadership gap. He had a clarity gap.

You've already met David Chen, the sharp, respected CTO of a fast-scaling SaaS company. Technical? Absolutely. Trusted? No question. But something was still off. He didn't have a leadership gap. He had a clarity gap. He wasn't building a future. He was patching the present.

Every time a new fire popped up, David jumped in. A critical customer issue? He'd personally handle the root cause. A performance bottleneck? He'd take over the standup. He thought being indispensable meant being visible in the details.

But the more he jumped in, the slower the system moved. People stopped making decisions. Directors waited for his nod. Projects started dragging, not because of complexity, but because David had become the final checkpoint for everything. From the outside, it looked like a CTO in control, but on the inside, he was stuck operating like the engineering manager he used to be, just with a bigger team and more work.

In a coaching session, I asked him, "What do you think your actual job is now?" He said, "To make sure everything gets done right."

That's where the work started. I didn't correct him. I just paused and asked, "What happens when you're not there to make sure?"

He sat with that. Then, finally he said, "It probably falls apart." That's when the shift clicked.

"Exactly," I said. "So maybe the job now isn't to execute flawlessly, it's to build a system that doesn't collapse without you." That landed, not because it was brand new, but because he was ready to see it.

Over the next 90 days, David started shifting, not just what he did, but how he saw himself. He built a scoreboard so his team could track performance without waiting for updates. (Not a dashboard, a scoreboard. There's a difference. We'll get to that in chapter 8.) He mapped ownership clearly, so directors didn't default back to him. He shifted his 1-on-1s from checklists to strategy sessions. He stopped solving, and started coaching.

His work became more invisible, but his impact didn't. The CEO pulled him aside after a board meeting and said, "Whatever you're doing, it's changing the game around here. I hope it's viral. We could use a whole lot more of it."

David hadn't added more hours. He had added altitude. He didn't just level up his behavior. He rewired his identity. No longer was he just the operator who gets things done. He became the architect who makes sure the right things get done, even when he's not in the room.

Coach's Commentary

If your first instinct is to jump back in and fix it yourself, that's not leadership, it's muscle memory, and it's one of the hardest habits to break.

Presence + Ownership Mirror

You don't get strategic by reading more leadership books. You get strategic by noticing how you show up, especially when no one's watching.

Every leader has a presence, whether they've built it on purpose or not. The question is: Is yours sending the signal you want it to?

Take a look at the moments that define your week: the 1-on-1 where your direct report hesitates before making a decision, the leadership meeting where your ideas land, but only after someone else repeats them, the "quick check-in" that turns into you redoing someone's work.

What's the through-line in those moments?

Presence isn't about being the loudest in the room. It's about how you carry your clarity and hold your authority. It's the difference between offering input and setting direction, between making suggestions and moving decisions forward.

Here's where it gets uncomfortable: We often reinforce a brand we never actually chose.

If your strength is reliability, you might be seen as the dependable pair of hands, not the driver of vision. If you lead with collaboration, you might be the glue, quietly critical, but not the one setting direction. If you're the fixer, you might be training your team to bring you everything.

These reputations form fast, and they stick. Especially when you're good. So, ask yourself: *What do people count on me for? What assumptions do they make about what I want to own, or don't? What do I reinforce when I say yes too fast, or stay quiet too long?*

This isn't about changing who you are. It's about owning how you show up and making sure your presence matches your purpose. Because if your brand doesn't reflect your leadership, you'll keep getting invited to the wrong conversations, and you'll keep wondering why the room doesn't see what you already know about yourself.

Coach's Commentary

Your presence trains your team. If you hesitate, they wait. If you show up like the decision-maker, they move with you.

The Impact Ladder Grid

I've seen way too many leaders leading from at least one rung below where they actually are. They've earned trust, built systems, and carry real influence, but still act like they need permission. They jump in to fix instead of stepping back to design. That's not about ego, it's about misalignment.

This ladder isn't about your title. It's about your mindset. Each rung reflects a different level of leadership presence, ownership, and altitude. As you move up, your perspective expands. You stop reacting and start shaping. You stop carrying it all and start coaching others to carry with you. The ladder gives you a language for where you are, and a way to ask: *What would it look like to lead one level higher, starting this week?*

You can't change what you don't name. Most of the leaders I work with aren't stuck. They're underplaying. They're capable of more, and likely expected to lead at a higher level, and it's time they claimed that space. To make that visible, I use a tool called the Impact Ladder Grid. It's not a hierarchy. It's a mirror. Each rung reflects a different level of leadership presence, mindset, and responsibility. Take a look, and ask yourself honestly: *Where am I actually operating from? And where should I be?*

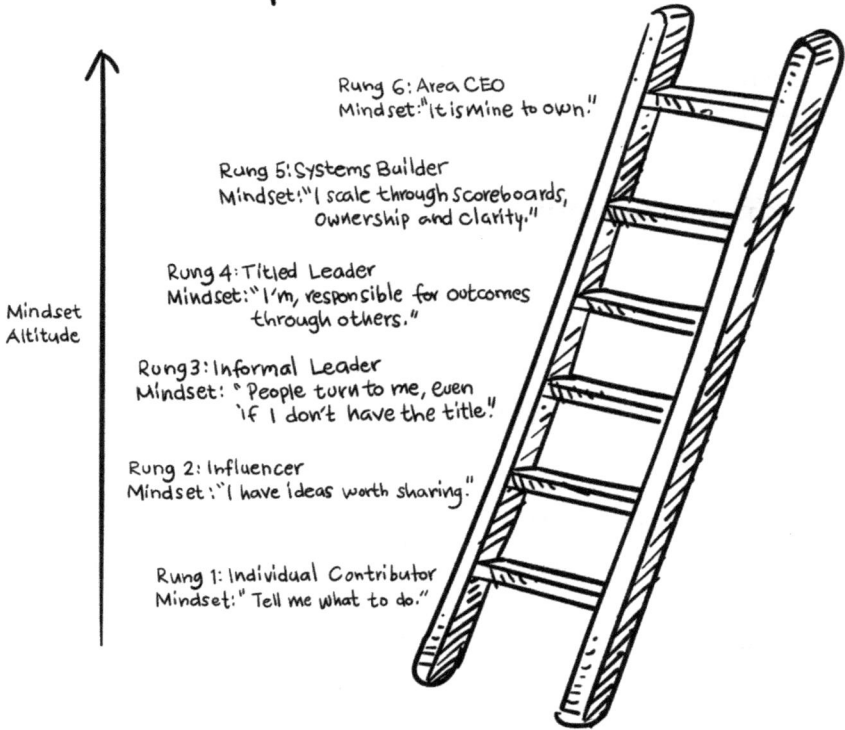

Impact = Altitude

Mindset Altitude

Rung 6: Area CEO
Mindset: "It is mine to own."

Rung 5: Systems Builder
Mindset: "I scale through scoreboards, ownership and clarity."

Rung 4: Titled Leader
Mindset: "I'm responsible for outcomes through others."

Rung 3: Informal Leader
Mindset: "People turn to me, even if I don't have the title."

Rung 2: Influencer
Mindset: "I have ideas worth sharing."

Rung 1: Individual Contributor
Mindset: "Tell me what to do."

Rung 1: Individual Contributor

Mindset: *Tell me what to do.*
You execute tasks well. You take direction and you deliver reliably, but you're deep in the weeds and don't yet see the broader system.

Rung 2: Influencer

Mindset: *I have ideas worth sharing.*
You shape thinking. You bring insights and you influence decisions without owning them, but your impact still depends on other people taking action.

Rung 3: Informal Leader

Mindset: *People turn to me, even if I don't have the title.*
You guide the team, connect the dots, and fill the gaps. However, because you lack formal authority, or you don't use it, you lead without leverage.

Rung 4: Titled Leader

Mindset: *I'm responsible for outcomes through others.*
You have the team and you have the mandate, but if you're still solving everything yourself, you're dragging the system instead of designing it.

Rung 5: System Builder

Mindset: *I scale through scoreboards, ownership, and clarity.*
You delegate, you coach, and you build systems that move without your direct involvement. But now the work shifts from doing tasks to shaping culture and performance through others.

Rung 6: Area CEO

Mindset: *This is mine to own.*
You lead with strategic autonomy. You act like the CEO of your function, your domain, your world, your area. You build momentum and trust that lasts, and you don't ask for permission. You operate like the outcome depends on you, because it does.

You might be ready and expected to operate at a higher level, but you're still leading like you're a rung or two (or three) below. You've got the trust, the scope, the expectations. Your boss is waiting for you to own it. But if you keep softening your voice, overexplaining decisions, and asking for permission you already have, you'll continue solving instead of shaping, waiting instead of deciding, and contributing instead of owning.

If you've been operating like the go-to person for everything, you're already a leader. Now the question is: What level are you leading from, and what would change if you stepped up one rung?

Tanya Brooks Wasn't Looking to Make Waves

She was the Acting COO of a fast-growing tech company, technically "holding down the fort" while the CEO decided whether to post the role externally. But unofficially? She was already running the show. She managed the senior leadership team. She was deep in cross-functional strategy. She pulled people out of silos, settled disputes, built budgets, and stabilized operations after a bumpy product launch. It wasn't a placeholder role. It was a pressure-cooker.

But you wouldn't have known it from how she showed up.

Tanya was operating like a Titled Leader on paper, but still thinking like an Informal Leader in practice. She qualified every idea. Softened every statement. She prefaced decisions with "if leadership agrees" and proposals with "just a thought." Her work was sharp. Her judgment was sound. Her instincts were solid. But she hadn't claimed the seat. She thought she was being respectful, waiting for the formal nod, honoring the hierarchy. But all it did was signal hesitation. And hesitation, at that level, reads as uncertainty.

Then came the moment that cracked it open.

In an executive meeting, Tanya laid out a strategy to streamline operations across three business units. Clear. Data-backed. Actionable. The room nodded along, then one of her peers rephrased her same proposal in more assertive terms... and the group jumped on board like it was a fresh idea. Tanya didn't fight it. But she noticed. And in our next coaching session, she brought it up.

"I just don't want to overstep," she said.

"But Tanya," I asked, "aren't you already doing the job?"

She hesitated. Then admitted: "Yeah... I guess I am."

And that was the shift. She didn't demand anything. She didn't launch a campaign for the title. She just started leading like the seat was hers. She made decisions without disclaimers. She showed up with presence. She stopped couching her impact behind soft language and started claiming her space.

She didn't demand the title.

She didn't launch a campaign.

She simply led like it was already hers.

And when that shift became undeniable, well, let's just say the title started catching up.

Coach's Commentary

People follow clarity. You don't need louder ideas. You need cleaner ownership.

Your Strength Isn't the Problem, Your Story About It Might Be

Let's talk about strengths. Not the buzzword kind. Not the kind that show up on annual reviews in tidy boxes like "communication" or "team player." I mean the ones that drive how you operate when no one's looking.

Maybe you're the fixer. The stabilizer. The workhorse. The unshakable calm in a sea of chaos. Maybe your superpower is knowing exactly what to say in a room full of tension or being five steps ahead of a problem no one else saw coming.

Those are real. They matter. But they can also become limits if you don't see them clearly.

Strengths don't scale when you over-identify with them. That's when your brand starts shrinking instead of expanding. The fixer becomes the bottleneck. The workhorse becomes the crutch. The connector becomes the glue that holds the team, but never leads it.

You start telling yourself, "This is just what I'm good at," and then you stop reaching for the parts of leadership that would stretch you further. But here's the thing: If your strength doesn't evolve, your leadership won't either. The reputation that got you here won't always be the one that gets you to what's next. At some point, you stop being seen as the high performer and start being seen as the always-available problem solver.

That's not a promotion path. That's a ceiling. So, here's what I want you to ask:

- What do people rely on me for? Is that what I want to be known for?

- Am I using my best leadership strengths, or hiding behind them because they feel safer than visibility?

- When I enter a room, what kind of presence do I bring? What kind of presence do I want to bring?

If you're not leading with intention, you're leading by default. And default doesn't build credibility. It just builds inertia. The goal isn't to change who you are. It's to stretch into the version of your leadership that reflects where you want to operate, not just where you've always been valued.

Leadership Challenge Anchor: Step 1—Introspection

This chapter is the beginning of your Six-Step Leadership Challenge, and it starts where all real leadership begins, not with a plan, but with a mirror.

Step 1—Introspection requires you to name the truth of how you lead right now:

- What do you already carry?

- Where do you operate from?

- How do you show up, intentionally or not?

It's not soft work, but it's essential work because until you see yourself clearly, you can't lead clearly. The rest of the steps, systems, strategy, culture, experiments, build on this, but none of it sticks if you skip this step.

Leadership that lasts always starts here.

Driving Question:

☞ What do you already own, and what would it look like to lead it one rung higher?

Your Coaching Question From Jim:

☞ If someone shadowed your leadership for a week, what would they say you lead? And what would they say you're still waiting to claim?

Mini Challenge: Claim It

✎ Download Worksheet: W1 – Own Your Area Map

You may have started this list back in the introduction, but if not, now's the time. Make a full inventory of everything you touch, shape, or influence. Projects. Decisions. Outcomes. Teams. Relationships. Systems. This isn't about job titles; it's about leadership gravity.

Then look at that list and ask: *Am I running these? Or reacting inside them? Am I solving? Or shaping?*

That's the moment the shift begins.

Final Reframe: Leadership Isn't Granted. It's Claimed.

You're not waiting for a title. You're not waiting for permission. You're not waiting for someone in a higher box on the org chart to say, "Now you're allowed to lead differently."

You're already doing it.

But invisible leadership doesn't scale. Helpful doesn't build momentum. Quiet doesn't shape culture. You already own more than you realize. Now it's time to own how you show up inside it. Because leadership isn't just about what you hold. It's about how you move.

☞ If you remember nothing else from this chapter, remember this:

Leadership doesn't start when someone else names it. It starts when you do. And once you've claimed it, there's a deeper question waiting: What happens when that voice in your head starts second-guessing you?

That's where we're headed next. Let's go.

CHAPTER 2

Kill the Firefighter Reflex:
Stop Leading From Fear

*If you're still fixing what others should own,
you're not a leader; you're a very expensive Band-Aid.*

– Jim Saliba

You weren't hired to hold it all together. You were hired to build what comes next.

You're exhausted, and not just from the hours. It's the kind of deep, draining fatigue that comes from carrying too much for too long while trying to hold the whole machine together: your team, your timelines, your boss, your reputation. You keep telling yourself it'll ease up eventually, but it won't. Not until you stop leading on autopilot.

Let's call it what it is, firefighting. You're jumping in, fixing things, saving the day, keeping the plates spinning. It looks helpful, and it feels necessary. But it's not. Because what starts as helpful eventually becomes harmful, keeping you in motion but out of leadership.

You didn't wake up one day and say, "I think I'll become a bottleneck." You just kept reacting, one decision at a time, one Slack ping at a time, one fire at a time, and before you knew it, you were in the middle of everything, without actually leading any of it.

Coach's Commentary

Firefighting is emotional busywork. It looks productive. It feels noble. But it's the enemy of anything that actually scales.

The Four Leadership Fears (That Keep Smart People Stuck)

You're not firefighting because you're broken. You're firefighting because something deeper in you, some core leadership reflex, is trying to keep you safe, valuable, or in control.

These reflexes don't come out of nowhere. They're built on fear. Beneath every overreaction is a reflex, and beneath every reflex is a fear. The fear of failing. The fear of being exposed. The fear of not being enough. The fear of being too much.

Over the years, in thousands of coaching hours, I've seen the same patterns emerge again and again. And they're not random. They're reflexes powered by fear. In a recent survey, 95 percent of leaders said they regularly operate from one or more of the following reflexes, especially in moments of stress, urgency, or change. These are the four leadership fears I've named, coached, and taught for years. They're not just personal; they're systemic, and if left unexamined, they quietly hijack how we show up. Let's name them.

1. Fear of Incompetence *(aka Impostor Syndrome)*

What if I don't actually know what I'm doing?

This fear erodes confidence from the inside out. You overfunction to compensate, staying late, saying yes to everything, and double-checking what you already know how to do. Even with the title, you feel one mistake away from being exposed. It's not a lack of skill. It's the belief that your credibility is conditional.

This often shows up as hesitation and decision delay, ping-ponging between priorities while searching for perfect answers, slowing projects while you gather "just one more piece of data." The message your team receives is: "We need to be perfect before we move." This builds a culture of hesitation and overcaution, where progress stalls, decisions drag, and no one wants to be first.

2. Fear of Looking Foolish

If I speak up and I'm wrong, they'll never trust me again.

You second-guess. You wait. You bury ideas until they're bulletproof, and then it's too late. You default to consensus, cling to process, and defer to past practice, even when you know it's outdated. It's the safe bet, even if it doesn't work anymore.

The message your team receives is: "Play it safe. Don't take risks. Don't stand out." This builds a culture of conformity and excessive conservatism, where creativity dies, innovation flatlines, and people stick to old processes even when they no longer serve.

3. Fear of Failure

If this goes wrong, it's on me.

You micromanage. You hesitate. You over-engineer the plan. One more draft. One more check-in. One more contingency. Not because you're indecisive, but because the stakes feel too high to trust momentum. So you delay, delegate upward, or push decisions outward, anywhere but yourself, so there's someone to blame if it fails.

The message your team receives: "If you mess this up, you're on your own." This builds a culture of blame and dependency, where decisions get passed around endlessly, ownership gets fuzzy, and no one wants to claim risk.

4. Fear of Vulnerability

If I don't have it all together, they'll lose confidence in me.

You keep the mask on. You present the polished version. You power through with composure while silently running on fumes. You avoid asking for help, sharing real challenges, or giving tough feedback because you fear rejection or criticism. But that armor creates distance.

The message your team receives is: "Don't bring problems. Don't show weakness. Keep it together, no matter what." This builds a culture of mistrust and passive-aggressive avoidance, where real issues go underground and surface-level harmony replaces honest feedback.

These fears aren't just emotional. They're cultural, and if left unchecked, they will ripple through your team, your function, and your company. Before long, they don't just shape how you lead, they define your entire operating system.

Now that the four fears are on the table, let's unpack how they start to shape your leadership when left unaddressed. Because fear doesn't just freeze us. It drives us. It fuels reflexes that feel helpful in the moment, but quietly erode trust, ownership, and momentum over time. Here's what you're about to see in each reflex:

First, the core behavior, the move you make automatically when pressure hits.

Second, the fear behind it, what your brain is trying to protect you from.

Third, the blind spot, the cost you don't see until it's already spread.

And finally, the leadership cost, the ripple effect that slows your team, your progress, and your impact.

Let's take a look.

Meet Your Reflex

These patterns aren't random; they're reflexes. Each is powered by fear, shaped by experience, and strengthened every time you use it to feel safe, capable, or in control. If you want to see why you lead the way you do, start here: You're not broken, you're just patterned.

Plenty of sharp leaders I coach have one of these dominant reflexes that kicks in when things get hard. You probably do too. These reflexes often start as strengths: quick action, deep expertise, strong drive. But in times of stress, they become survival mechanisms, and survival doesn't scale.

Each reflex is tied to a deeper fear. Left unchecked, they don't just slow you down; they stall your climb up the leadership ladder. The higher you go, the more your team mirrors your mindset, and the more you lead from reflex, the harder it is to operate at the rung you're truly ready for.

There are plenty of other reflexes out there, each shaped by different experiences and pressures. But these four show up again and again in the leaders I coach. They're the patterns that don't just slow you down, they reshape your team's behavior and set the cultural tone, whether you mean for them to or not.

Now let's look more closely at each of the four common reflexes.

The Overthinker (or The Perfectionist)

You slow things down. You question everything. You double-check, triple-check, and keep decisions on hold until you're sure. It feels like diligence. It feels like quality. But underneath it all is the fear that if you move too soon or too imperfectly, you'll be exposed as not good enough.

You overprepare, fill in every gap, anticipate every objection, and seek the perfect plan before acting. You might even pause one project to work on another while you "figure it out," ping-ponging your focus so you can avoid the risk of being wrong.

To your team, it doesn't look like care. It looks like hesitation. It feels like permission to wait. Decisions stall, momentum dies, and what you think of as protecting quality actually protects inaction. Over time, this creates a culture of delay and second-guessing. Your team mirrors you. They overplan, underdecide, and avoid committing until they have every answer. Progress slows to the speed of your certainty. What started as caution becomes a bottleneck. And you don't just slow your own growth, you teach your team that safety is more important than movement.

Driven by: Fear of incompetence

Blind spot: Perfection becomes paralysis

Message to the team: "We can't move until it's perfect."

Leadership cost: Slowed momentum, delayed projects, and a culture of hesitation and overanalysis.

David's Relapse

David, our CTO of a fast-scaling SaaS company, had done the work. He delegated more. He created scoreboards. He empowered his leaders to own decisions. He had moved into Architect mode, finally leading from the top of the ladder.

But pressure has a way of dragging us backward.

During a high-stakes customer escalation, the product team missed a critical deadline. The stakes felt too high for mistakes. While David didn't jump in to fix it himself, he did start managing it to death. He called extra review meetings, revised timelines and requirements multiple times, and insisted on approving every decision before anything moved forward, not because he didn't trust his team's skill, but because he couldn't risk missing something. He wanted certainty. He wanted proof. He needed to know nothing would be missed that would expose him, or the company, as being unprepared.

In our next session, he shook his head. "I know I shouldn't have," he said. "But I kept thinking if I didn't catch it, no one would. I couldn't afford that mistake."

It wasn't arrogance. It was the fear of being incompetent. David's reflex was to slow things down for safety. But in trying to prevent errors, he created new ones. Momentum died. Decisions stalled. His team lost confidence, not in themselves, but in their freedom to lead.

David's Ladder Check

David generally operates at Rung 6, Area CEO, with clear systems and empowered leaders. But when things got tense, he slipped back to Rung 4, Titled Leader, reviewing and controlling instead of shaping. His next move wasn't to work harder; it was to recognize his fear reflex, rebuild trust, and return to Architect mode, where his value came from designing systems that moved without him.

The Avoider

You keep things safe. You lean on proven processes and standard practices even when they no longer fit. Not because you're careless, but because you don't want to suggest something that might fail. You stick to precedent, cling to what has worked before, and avoid proposing bold shifts. When someone asks for new ideas, you defer, saying, "Let's do what we know works." It feels cautious and responsible, but it kills momentum.

This fear doesn't always look like silence. It looks like endless caution, checklists, and well-worn paths. You avoid risk by choosing certainty over innovation. You second-guess the new approach because you don't want to look foolish if it fails. But here's the cost: Your team learns to avoid risk, too. They wait for permission or precedent. Innovation stalls, creative thinking flatlines, and everyone learns to stay inside the lines, even when those lines no longer lead anywhere.

You're not just avoiding mistakes. You're training your team to play it safe. In a fast-changing world, that isn't prudence. It's a liability.

Driven by: Fear of appearing foolish

Blind spot: Safety feels responsible, but it stalls progress

Message to the team: "Let's stick to what we know."

Leadership cost: Conformity, stalled innovation, and lost momentum.

Michael's Silent Signal

Michael was a Senior Director in a global logistics firm. He was calm, methodical, and deeply respected. He wasn't loud, but he was usually right. But lately, he was coasting on process. In meetings, he nodded along. He rarely challenged the plan. Even when it was clear the direction needed a rethink, he defaulted to consensus. His peers started calling him "reliably safe." But that wasn't a compliment. It was a warning.

In one session, I asked what was holding him back. He said, "I don't want to derail things. Or worse, suggest something that turns out to be wrong." That's the reflex, the fear of appearing foolish. Michael wasn't lazy. He was filtering himself so carefully that his leadership stopped showing up. And in that vacuum, projects he should have shaped moved forward without him.

He didn't need louder volume. He needed braver presence.

Michael's Ladder Check

Michael was *expected* to operate at Rung 4, Titled Leader, with clear ownership and visible direction. But he was *showing up* more like Rung 3, Informal Leader, cautious, behind the scenes, and overly edited.

Although he wants to go right to Rung 5, System builder, he first needs to stabilize at Rung 4, owning decisions clearly and leading conversations publicly. Once that foundation is strong, he can then stretch toward Rung 5, where he designs systems that move without him and scales his leadership impact.

The Fixer (or The Hero)

You jump in fast. You know how to solve things. For most of your career, that's what earned you trust. But now you're still doing too much yourself, not because you want control, but because you're afraid of what happens if you don't. You feel responsible for protecting the team, the customer, and the outcome, so you take on more than you should. You micromanage. You over-engineer. You hesitate to let go. And here's the real tell: You deflect decisions, pushing them up, out, or back so that if something goes wrong, it won't land on you. It feels like you're shielding everyone. It feels responsible. But it actually slows them down, kills ownership, and teaches them to wait.

Over time, this builds a quiet dysfunction. You become the bottleneck you were trying to avoid. Decisions stall, momentum dies, and your team learns that safety means waiting for you. Your vigilance becomes the risk, and what started as protecting them becomes controlling them. Eventually, you're not just carrying too much, you're building a culture of hesitation and dependency that centers everything around you.

Driven by: Fear of failure

Blind spot: Protecting everyone else creates dependency

Message to the team: "You're not ready. I'll handle it."

Leadership cost: Slowed momentum, delayed decisions, blame-shifting, and a team that won't move without you.

Tonya's Overload Moment

Tonya wasn't trying to control everything. She was trying to avoid getting it wrong.

As Acting COO, she'd stepped into a role no one had officially handed her, and no one was fully supporting. The CEO was "still exploring options," the org was stretched thin, and another crisis seemed to hit every week.

So, Tonya did what she'd always done. She stepped in, rechecked timelines, rewrote decks, and sat in on vendor calls "just to be safe." Projects piled up on her desk, not because her team couldn't handle them, but because she was afraid of letting anything fall through the cracks.

"It's not that I don't trust them," she said. "I just can't afford to miss something."

But it wasn't about trust. It was about her fear of being the one who dropped the ball. What she couldn't see yet was the ripple effect. Her team was slowing down, not out of confusion, but caution. They'd learned to wait for her green light. Her vigilance had become their bottleneck.

The clarity came when one of her senior directors finally asked, "Do you want us to move forward, or wait for your edits?"

It wasn't a critique. It was a reflection. And Tonya saw it.

Tonya's Ladder Check

Tonya is operating at Rung 4, Titled Leader, owning results through her team but still managing everything herself, and acting as the constant go-to without the structure to scale. Her real move isn't to keep absorbing more, it's to start thinking like a System Builder, designing the structure, delegation, and rhythms that let her team move without waiting on her. That's how she stabilizes at Rung 4 and then grows into Rung 5, where she leads through systems, not sheer effort.

The Overachiever

You say yes to everything, you do more than anyone, and for much of your career, that's what made you valuable. You won through sheer effort and earned trust by being the one who always delivered. But underneath that hustle is fear. Not fear of the work, but fear of being seen as anything less than capable. Fear that if you drop the ball or show cracks, people will question your credibility.

So, you armor up. You stay late, absorb the slack, and make sure nobody sees you sweat. You present the polished version while quietly running on fumes. It feels noble. It feels protective. It feels like leadership. But the cost is hidden and corrosive.

You're not just carrying too much, you're teaching your team to carry too little. When you overfunction, they underfunction. They learn that the real decisions, the hard calls, the messy parts of ownership will land with you in the end. So they wait, and over time, this builds a culture of passivity and surface-level trust. Everyone stays polite, professional, and distant. The hard conversations don't happen, feedback goes underground, and while everything looks fine on the outside, the real issues stay buried.

You don't just exhaust yourself. You shrink your team's growth while erasing your own.

Driven by: Fear of vulnerability

Blind spot: Protecting everyone else hides your own cracks, and theirs

Message to the team: "I've got it all under control. You don't need to worry."

Leadership cost: Burnout, mistrust, and stalled development (yours and your team's).

Sarah's Disappearing Act

Sarah was a Senior Manager of Strategy and Growth at a fast-moving consulting and finance firm. She wasn't just a strong performer; she was the glue. When things broke, Sarah fixed them. When people slipped, Sarah caught them. She held the team together quietly, powerfully, and almost invisibly.

But that was the problem. She wasn't building a leadership brand. She was holding up the walls. She didn't say no. Ever. She picked up projects that weren't hers, jumped into deliverables at the last minute, and absorbed the pressure of two levels above her because it felt easier than letting something fall. Her calendar was full, her inbox was chaos, and her team? They were floundering without feedback because Sarah was always three layers deep in someone else's crisis.

In one of our sessions, she finally said, "I feel like I'm doing everything, and somehow still failing everyone."

She wasn't, but she *was* disappearing. The more she overfunctioned, the less her leadership was visible, and the more she avoided vulnerability, the harder it became to delegate, coach, or lead with presence.

Sarah wasn't just busy. She was locked into a value system that cost her more than time.

Sarah's Ladder Check

Sarah is operating at Rung 2, Influencer, with clear impact but no formal leverage through her team. She needs to claim Rung 3 by shifting from doing everything herself to guiding, supporting, and empowering others. As she strengthens those skills, she can move into Rung 4, where she manages outcomes through her team rather than carrying them alone. Only then can she begin building the systems and structures of Rung 5, where leadership becomes scalable and self-sustaining.

Quick Map of the Four Reflexes		
Fear	**Reflex**	**Dysfunction**
Fear of Failure "I can't risk mistakes that will be on me."	The Fixer (or The Hero) Jump in fast, control the work, and push decisions elsewhere so I don't own the risk	Team waits on you, decision flow stalls, culture of blame.
Fear of Incompetence "I'm not good enough, I might be found out."	The Overthinker (or Perfectionist) Perfection becomes paralysis	Team slows down, momentum stalls, culture of hesitation.
Fear of Appearing Foolish "If I'm wrong, I'll lose credibility."	The Avoider Hold back ideas, stick to what's safe, and avoid bold moves	Team plays it safe, innovation stalls, culture of conformity.
Fear of Vulnerability "I can't let anyone see cracks or doubt."	The Overachiever Overfunction, say yes to everything, and polish the image so no one sees stress	Team stays passive, avoids ownership, culture of mistrust.

The Cost Isn't Just Personal, It's Cultural

These reflexes don't stay contained. They ripple, they spread, and they quietly shape the culture around you, whether you mean for them to or not, because when you lead from fear, your team feels it. When you default to overcontrol, hesitation, overwork, or silence, they start doing the same.

And here's the danger leaders often overlook: Fear-based reflexes, when repeated long enough, don't just create short-term friction; they create long-term dysfunction. What starts as a coping mechanism becomes a leadership pattern. What starts as a leadership pattern becomes a cultural norm. And what starts as a cultural norm becomes damn hard to undo.

Your instinct to help, protect, prove, or control, left unchecked, becomes the blueprint your team builds around. It limits how people speak up, it shapes how decisions are made, and it defines what "safe" looks like.

You may not feel it right away. But culture has a memory, and the longer fear runs the show, the harder it becomes to rebuild trust, accountability, and autonomy.

Coach's Commentary

Fear is contagious. But so is clarity. The culture you're leading *right now* is either mirroring your default or rising because of your design.

From Doer to Architect: Stop Holding It Together. Start Designing What Comes Next.

You didn't ask to get stuck in the weeds; you just kept getting rewarded for being helpful. You solved problems fast, you picked up the slack, you filled the gaps, and you made things run. And people noticed, so they gave you more. You got promoted to lead, but you never stopped doing.

You're still solving things manually, still reacting to chaos, still trying to hold the whole machine together by sheer force of will.

That's not leadership. That's burnout with a title.

If you want to lead at the next level, you need a different kind of motion, because leadership doesn't scale through effort, it scales through elevation.

We've already covered the Impact Ladder, the internal mindset shift. Now we'll name the external one: How you actually spend your time.

Rungs 1 and 2: The Doer

You get stuff done, you knock out tasks, you influence from the edges. But everything depends on you being in the mix, and your impact ends when you clock out. You're inside the system, reacting to it, not shaping it.

Rungs 3 and 4: The Manager

You coordinate, you delegate, you manage output through other people. You're still deep in the day-to-day, running approvals, checking drafts, and nudging timelines. You're trying to drive the train while riding it, and eventually, something's going to derail.

Rungs 5 and 6: The Architect

You stop chasing problems and start designing systems. You lead through clarity, not control. You make it easier for people to do great work without you standing over their shoulders. Your value isn't in how much you do, it's in what works when you're not there.

The Impact Shift

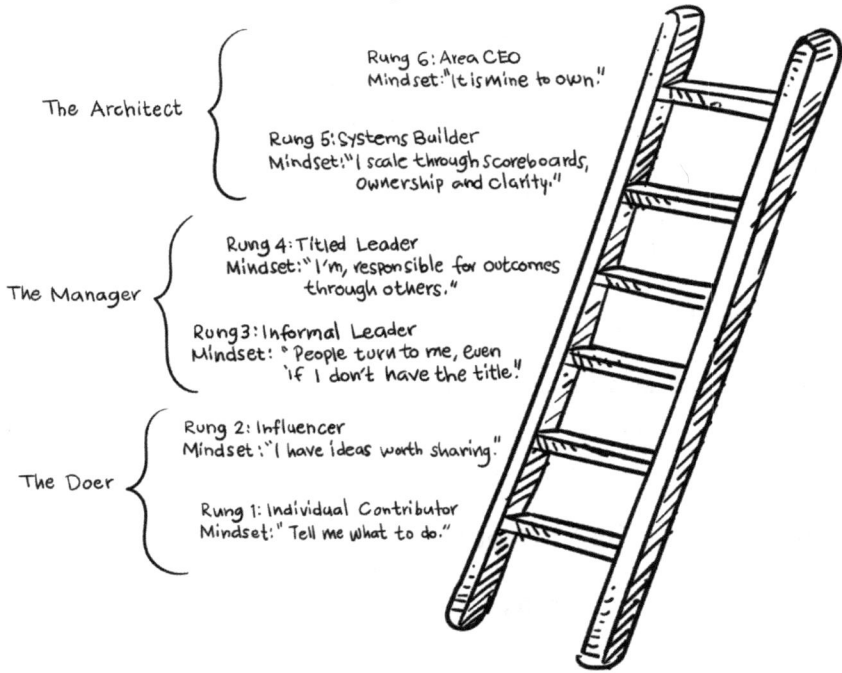

The Architect
{
Rung 6: Area CEO
Mindset: "It is mine to own."

Rung 5: Systems Builder
Mindset: "I scale through scoreboards, ownership and clarity."
}

The Manager
{
Rung 4: Titled Leader
Mindset: "I'm, responsible for outcomes through others."

Rung 3: Informal Leader
Mindset: "People turn to me, even if I don't have the title."
}

The Doer
{
Rung 2: Influencer
Mindset: "I have ideas worth sharing."

Rung 1: Individual Contributor
Mindset: "Tell me what to do."
}

Too many promotions happen without a mindset shift, so the title changes, but the altitude stays the same. They're still operating like Doers, just with a nicer title and a more crowded calendar. Some move into Manager mode, but they're managing activity, not impact. Very few make the leap to Architect, where leadership actually scales.

It's not your company holding you back. It's the reflexes you haven't questioned, and the patterns you've normalized. You can lead from higher up the ladder, but you have to stop treating busyness like a badge.

Coach's Commentary

If every decision still flows through you, your team isn't learning; they're waiting.

Leadership isn't about how much you carry. It's about what moves without you. That's the standard. That's the shift. And that's where we're headed next.

Driving Question:

Where are you still solving problems manually instead of designing systems that solve them without you?

Your Coaching Question From Jim:

Which reflex do you see in yourself when pressure hits, and what's one step you could take to break that pattern?

Mini Challenge: The Firefighting Audit

You can't shift what you haven't named. So, for the next five workdays, start logging every fire that pulls you off-course. No judgment, just the facts:

- What blew up?

- Who pulled you in?

- How did you react?

Then at the end of the week, ask yourself:

- Was this actually mine to fix, or did I default into it?

- Was it urgent, or just poorly scoped?

- What could have prevented it?

- Who else could have handled it with the right system or support?

Here's a sample breakdown:

The Fire	Was It Mine?	Why Was It Urgent?	What Would've Prevented It?	Who Else Could've Handled It?
Launch deck redlines at 9 p.m.	No, pulled in because approvals were skipped	Client review the next morning	QA checklist + reviewer roles	Team lead + product owner (if empowered)

Once you've logged your week, do one thing: Pick a fire and kill it at the source.

- Update the process.

- Set a boundary or guardrail.

- Shift the ownership.

- Or, if it's not critical, let it burn.

You are not here to be the safety net. You're here to build the net and teach others how to use it.

✎ Download Worksheet: W2 – Firefighting Audit + System Design Canvas

Final Reframe: You Don't Scale by Solving. You Scale by Designing.

You're not here to be the fix. You're here to build what fixes things without you.

The leaders who make the biggest impact aren't the ones chasing every spark. They're the ones who design with intention, so their team, their culture, and their systems know how to move when they're not in the room. Architects don't rush to chaos; they architect what comes next.

Every time you put down the firehose and pick up the blueprint, you shift your altitude and your influence.

If you remember nothing else from this chapter, remember this:

You don't scale leadership by holding it all together. You scale it by letting go, on purpose.

Once you stop reacting, it's time to ask the deeper question: What kind of culture has been quietly growing while you've been busy putting out fires? This is where leadership begins to shift from motion to meaning. Let's go.

CHAPTER 3

Culture Is the Current Beneath

The real company values?
They live in what gets promoted, protected, or ignored.

– Jim Saliba

You're Not Leading in a Vacuum

You've got vision, a plan, and clear goals, but here's the thing no one tells you when you step into a bigger seat: You don't just lead people. You lead people inside a culture. And that culture? It moves first, every time. Before your plans. Before your strategy. Before your best intentions ever leave the starting gate.

If you don't learn to see it, you will get wrecked by it.

Leadership Challenge Anchor: Step 2 – Extrospection

Step 1 was about the mirror, seeing yourself clearly. Step 2? It's about lifting your eyes to the landscape you're leading inside. This is the second move in the Six-Step Leadership Challenge: Extrospection. It's the art of reading your environment with precision. Because strategy doesn't live in a vacuum. It lives in systems, in unspoken rules, in the everyday rhythms of who speaks up, who shuts down, and what gets rewarded when no one's looking.

If you don't learn to read those patterns, you'll lead like a tourist, well-meaning, maybe even inspiring, but not native to the terrain. And culture knows when it's being led by someone who doesn't speak its language.

Extrospection means knowing the difference between what people say and what they actually do. Between stated values and real behaviors. Between what the slide deck claims and what the side-eye in the hallway confirms.

Leadership isn't just what you bring. It's what you can shift, and you can't shift what you can't see.

Culture Isn't a Buzzword; It's the Current Under Everything

We're not talking about values posters or corporate mantras. Culture is what people feel but rarely name. It's the invisible current beneath every meeting, every decision, and every delay.

You see it in what gets spotlighted and what gets swept aside, in who speaks freely and who watches what they say, in how quickly people escalate and how slowly they take risks, in what gets air cover and what gets quietly buried.

It's not written down. It's absorbed, mirrored, and enforced every day by leaders, by peers, and by silence. And unless you are actively designing for it, culture will default to the strongest personality in the room, or the oldest wound in the system.

David's Culture Clash: Strategy Meets Static

Let's go back to David Chen, the sharp, scrappy CTO we've been following. He'd done the introspection work. He'd leveled up. He was leading more strategically, building systems, and coaching his directors instead of micromanaging them. So, when he launched a bold cross-functional initiative to streamline operations and accelerate delivery, he expected a little resistance. What he didn't expect was for the whole thing to stall out. And not because the idea was flawed, but because the culture was allergic to how he introduced it.

In our next coaching session, David was frustrated. He told me he had laid it out clearly in the leadership meeting. The plan made sense. He had the data. And yet... nothing. Just dead silence. Then his calendar started filling up with one-on-ones and "circling back" meetings. He felt like he'd poked a bear he didn't even know was in the room.

I asked what he thought had gotten triggered. He paused, considering it. Maybe he'd skipped a step, he said. He hadn't realized there was a rule for how ideas were supposed to be introduced.

"There probably isn't a written one," I said. "But was there an unwritten one?"

He thought about it, then nodded. Now that he reflected, he hadn't checked in with the usual players ahead of time. He'd figured if the idea was solid, it should stand on its own.

"And how'd that work?" I asked.

He smiled, a little sideways. He got it. That was the moment it clicked for him. His rollout hadn't failed because the strategy lacked clarity or value. It failed because it ignored the room it was stepping into. It violated an unspoken norm: Nothing big moves without early buy-in from the legacy voices.

David wasn't wrong. But his approach had disrupted a power structure he hadn't even noticed. That's the thing about culture: it's the undercurrent. It's below the surface, easy to miss. But the moment you step wrong, it pulls you under.

Coach's Commentary

Culture doesn't show up in slide decks. It shows up in resistance, silence, and sideways energy when the rules underneath aren't honored.

You can't lead above culture until you learn to see it. Right now, your job isn't to fix it. It's to map it.

The Five Cultural Signals You Can't Afford to Miss

If you want to lead smarter, you need to listen harder, because culture doesn't shout; it whispers. And too many leaders are too busy reacting to hear it.

These five cultural signals? They're not HR talking points; they're field diagnostics. Ignore them, and you'll keep wondering why your team hesitates, your peers stall, or your bold new ideas fizzle in the hallway. Let's break them down:

1. What Gets Rewarded Fastest?

Look at who gets the spotlight. That's the actual value system.

- Are people recognized for team wins or personal heroics?

- Do thoughtful planners get credit, or just the ones who sprint and ship?

- Who actually gets promoted, and why?

Say/Do Gap: "We value collaboration," but bonuses go to the lone closer, not the team that made the close possible. What gets rewarded becomes the unofficial playbook everyone follows, no matter what the posters on the wall say.

2. What Gets Punished Hardest

Not in policy, in practice.

- Are people quietly sidelined for challenging the status quo?

- Does speaking truth to power cost influence?

- Are the boldest ideas the first to get shot down?

Say/Do Gap: "We encourage innovation," but the last person who raised a controversial idea got branded as not a team player and lost their project. Punishment isn't always loud, but it's always instructional. People learn what's safe by watching who gets burned.

3. What Gets Ignored the Longest

Neglect is one of the most honest signals a culture gives off.

- Is burnout swept under the rug?

- Are bad actors tolerated because they deliver results?

- Do broken processes get patched again and again, but never fixed?

Say/Do Gap: "We hold people accountable," but deadlines slip, teams ghost follow-through, and no one calls it. What you ignore becomes culture, and once it's normalized, it becomes invisible.

4. Who Gets Promoted, and Why

You want to know what the company values? Watch who rises.

- Do promotions reward vision, or just endurance?

- Are servant leaders recognized, or just the ones who never say no?

- Is political navigation more important than impact?

Say/Do Gap: "We reward leadership," but the person who absorbed every fire drill and kept their head down got the nod, while the one who coached others and challenged norms got left behind. Promotion patterns are culture in disguise.

5. Where Conflict Goes

Every culture has conflict. The question is: where does it land?

- Are tough conversations had, or avoided?

- Does disagreement spark learning, or fear?

- Are teams trained to engage tension or navigate around it?

Say/Do Gap: "We value transparency," but feedback is sugarcoated, truth-tellers get labeled, and hard conversations only happen when something explodes. How conflict is handled tells you everything about trust.

Culture doesn't announce itself. It reveals itself through what people celebrate, avoid, ignore, protect, and promote. These five signals aren't just random observations; they're a diagnostic lens. When you learn to read them, you stop reacting to surface issues and start spotting the deeper forces that shape behavior. And once you see them clearly, you can finally lead inside them, intentionally, not accidentally. Let's look at what happened when Tonya missed one of those signals.

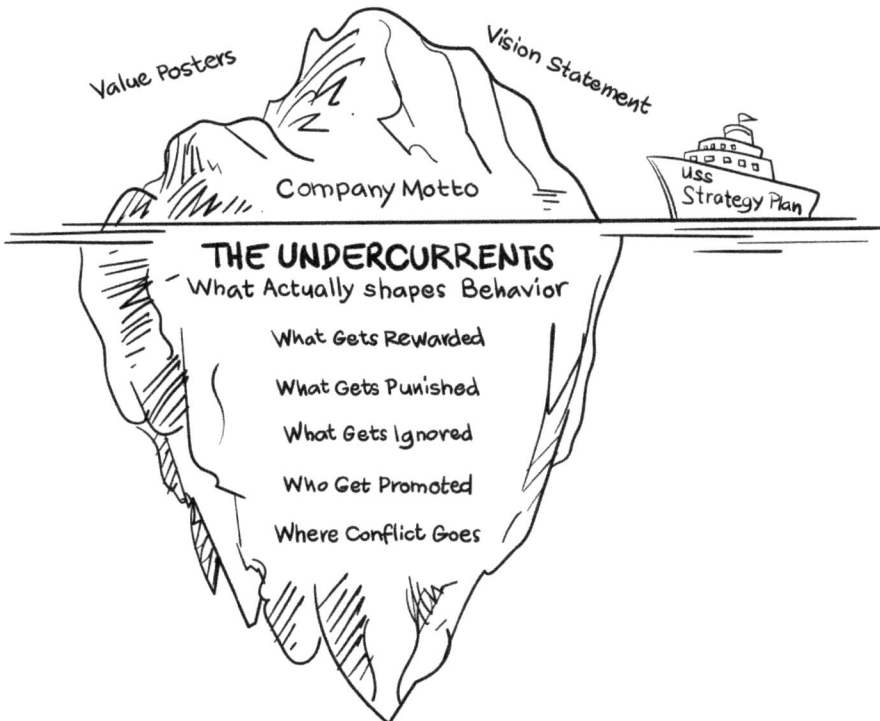

What the companies would like culture to be

Value Posters
Vision Statement
Company Motto
USS Strategy Plan

THE UNDERCURRENTS
What Actually shapes Behavior

What Gets Rewarded

What Gets Punished

What Gets Ignored

Who Get Promoted

Where Conflict Goes

Tanya's Culture Blind Spot

Tonya Brooks, still serving as Acting COO, had made real progress since our last conversation. She'd claimed her seat, tightened execution, and begun reshaping how her directors operated. The clarity was there, the intent was solid, but something still wasn't landing.

"They either fade out," she said during a coaching session, "or get quietly reversed when I'm not in the room."

I asked, "What current are you swimming in, and have you taken the time to read it, or just tried to swim through it?"

That stopped her, because Tonya hadn't read the current; she'd tried to force her way forward. She was leading with precision, but the org was still operating with caution, not because they didn't respect her, but because the culture didn't move that fast. Her strategy made sense, but her pace triggered resistance. She hadn't realized that the real rules weren't in her slide decks. They lived in backchannel approvals, hallway hesitations, and unspoken rituals that protected legacy norms.

So, we started mapping the signals:

- Which VPs and directors were stalling, and why?

- Where decisions kept "reopening" after alignment?

- What got airtime in meetings versus what actually moved after?

Tonya saw it. The issue wasn't her direction; it was her delivery. So, she slowed down without losing ground. She asked better questions before making harder calls. She created space for her directors to process the shift, rather than push past their uncertainty. She didn't stop driving change, she just synced her rhythm to the culture's current, and when she did, the resistance started to fade, the buy-in grew, and the changes finally stuck.

Coach's Commentary

You're not here to bulldoze the culture. You're here to learn its rhythm, then teach it a new one, beat by beat.

Behavior *Is* the Culture

Culture isn't a vibe. It's not a brand pillar or a perk list. It's not the values poster on the breakroom wall. Culture is whatever gets repeated when no one's watching. It's the quiet patterns that emerge when the pressure's on and the spotlight's off.

If people keep showing up late to meetings, the culture tolerates it. If managers stall hard conversations until performance review season, the culture trains avoidance. If applause only goes to fire-fighters, not planners, you're going to get more fire-fighting. None of this is malicious, it's just repetition. However, repetition becomes expectation, and expectation is culture in action.

You don't need to launch a culture campaign. You need to start reinforcing the behaviors that match the environment you want to lead.

- **Want a culture that tells the truth faster?** Be the one who says the hard thing first.

- **Want a culture that moves with clarity?** Start every meeting with what matters and end it with who's doing what by when.

- **Want a culture that values ownership?** Stop rescuing and start coaching.

> ## Coach's Commentary
>
> If you're not intentional about what you repeat, your habits will build a culture without your consent.

Driving Question

Where is the cultural current pulling hardest around you, and how is it shaping your leadership more than you realize?

Your Coaching Question From Jim

If someone shadowed your leadership this week, what would they say the culture actually values, based on what you respond to, reward, or ignore?

Mini Challenge: Culture Signals Audit

Download Worksheet: W3 – Culture Signals Audit

Spend 20 minutes doing a quick culture read inside your current team or org. For each of the five signals below, jot down the *actual* patterns you've noticed. Not what the handbook says, but what your gut says is true.

1. What gets rewarded fastest?

2. What gets punished hardest?

3. What gets ignored the longest?

4. Who gets promoted, and for what?

5. Where does conflict go?

Now look at your answers and ask:

- What am I reinforcing, intentionally or not?

- What am I tolerating?

- What's one small signal I could shift this week, by calling something out, naming a truth, or rewarding the behavior I want more of?

Culture doesn't shift because you have a new value statement. It shifts when you behave like the shift already matters.

Final Reframe

If you remember nothing else from this chapter, remember this:

Culture is the current beneath. If you can't see it, you can't lead it.

It's not what you say, it's what you allow, avoid, or quietly reward that sets the tone. And here's the real wake-up call: You're not just leading inside the culture. You're shaping it, whether you mean to or not.

But this is just the beginning, because beneath the current of culture lies something even more powerful: the machine itself. The structures, blockers, incentives, and power flows that decide what actually moves. If culture is the current, then Chapter 4 is the terrain. Strap in. We're going deeper.

CHAPTER 4

Map the Terrain

If your team keeps tripping on the same cracks, it's not a people problem. It's a terrain problem you haven't mapped yet.

– Jim Saliba

You're not stuck because you're wrong for the role. You're stuck because the *terrain* you're in isn't designed for what you're trying to do or build. This isn't about performance, or motivation, or finding the perfect productivity hack. You're stuck because you're leading inside an invisible framework that was rigged long before you got there. And unless you learn to see it, you'll keep slamming into walls that don't show up on the org chart: The calendar chaos. The rework. The way your most strategic ideas mysteriously stall while low-value fire drills get all the oxygen. That's not just culture. That's *terrain.*

Step 2 of the Six-Step Leadership Challenge isn't just about scanning for behaviors. It's about mapping the *terrain* that decides what actually moves, and what gets quietly buried: the rules, the rhythms, and the real levers of progress or paralysis. Because here's the shift: Culture whispers how to behave, but terrain determines what actually happens.

You're Not Just Fighting Culture, You're Fighting the Setup

In the last chapter, we tackled culture, the emotional current that drives behavior, belonging, and what feels safe to say out loud. But that's only half the equation.

You're not just working inside a culture, you're operating inside a system, and if you don't know how to tell the difference, you'll end up coaching what actually needs redesigning. You'll keep taking resistance personally when it's really structural. You'll solve the wrong problem faster. Let's break it down:

Culture is the emotional operating rules. This is what's expected. The vibe, the unspoken "shoulds," what feels safe, and what gets silently judged.

Terrain is the structural landscape. This is what's actually possible. It's what slows you down, and what lets you move, the incentives, the workflows, the power dynamics, and the unofficial alliances shaping what moves and what stalls. You can rally the team all you want, but if the system is rigged, your big ideas will still die in the hallway.

In our next example, Michael didn't miss the strategy; he missed the architecture it was trying to survive in.

From System Blindness to Strategic Seeing: Michael's Shift

You already met Michael Reynolds back in Chapter 2. He's the Senior Director of Operations, has a high EQ, is collaborative, and highly trusted. He's also a classic Avoider. Michael didn't like to push. He preferred alignment, consensus, and smooth handoffs over sharp elbows. And that worked, until it didn't.

He'd designed a beautifully clear execution framework: one view of progress, one weekly cadence, fewer dropped balls. Everyone nodded. Everyone agreed. And then… nothing. The momentum drained somewhere between the meeting and the inbox. In our next session, Michael was frustrated.

"Jim, I don't get it. I made it easy. It makes sense. No one disagreed. Why is this still stuck?"

I asked, "Michael, did you design this plan for the terrain you *wish* you were in, or the terrain you're actually navigating?"

That landed. He'd been solving for logic, not protection. He built a plan for a rational org, but he was operating in an overly cautious one. A system where firefighting was rewarded. Where metrics weren't shared unless they were flawless. Where cross-functional visibility felt like exposure, not progress. Michael hadn't failed. He just hadn't mapped the terrain. Once he did, he stopped trying to nudge the system gently and started designing moves that respected the constraints but didn't bow to them:

- He ran private alignment sessions with two legacy directors before anything hit the calendar.

- He shifted language from "new system" to "building on what's already working."

- He piloted with just two teams, letting the early wins speak louder than the pitch.

Michael didn't overhaul the structure, he just stopped shadowboxing, and that's when the system stopped pushing back.

Michael's Ladder Check

Michael had been operating from Rung 2, Influencer, skilled at soft power but avoiding direct friction. This move marked his transition to Rung 4, Titled Leader, where he was not just trusted but was making decisions and leading directly. His next shift? Stabilize there, and begin stretching toward Rung 5, where systems and strategy take the lead, not personality.

The Game You're in Runs on Politics, Not Org Charts

Influence doesn't live inside clean boxes and straight lines. It moves through living systems, politics, hidden alliances, turf wars, and quiet power plays that aren't written down anywhere but shape nearly every key decision.

David's Terrain Misread

You already know David Chen, the CTO who worked hard to rise to system-level leadership. He'd earned that spot by delegating decisions, empowering his team, and building the structures that let him lead at altitude. But even seasoned leaders get pulled back by reflex.

When his team scoped a cross-functional visibility initiative to improve delivery, David knew it would be sensitive. Finance would scrutinize controls. Marketing wanted to protect their narrative. Engineering valued sprint autonomy. He understood the politics he'd missed last time in the cultural undercurrent. But instead of mapping them, he tried to design around them in private. He overengineered the pitch, aiming to make it bulletproof. He kept delaying the rollout, convinced it wasn't ready, waiting for perfect alignment that was never coming. His reflex was overthinking and perfectionism. He kept refining, aiming to make the plan flawless before sharing it. The cost was losing momentum, because while he was polishing, the terrain was shifting under him. The exec team's priorities moved on, budget was allocated elsewhere, and the sense of urgency evaporated.

In our session, David named it himself.

"I was so focused on making it solid that I missed how fast the window was closing. I didn't see how little time I really had."

He hadn't read the terrain. He'd designed for a world where everyone had unlimited attention, aligned incentives, and patient timelines, but that wasn't the world he was leading in. David didn't fail because the idea was flawed; he failed because he didn't design it for the actual system it had to move through.

David's Ladder Check

David was operating at Rung 6, Area CEO, with system-level authority and strategic vision. But when the environment turned challenging, he slipped back to Rung 4, Manager, getting caught in reviews and sign-offs instead of designing forward.

His real move isn't just to regain altitude, but to hold it even when conditions get messy. That means sharing ideas before they're polished, making tradeoffs visible, and staying alert to the shifting terrain so he can adapt in real time. It means pausing before pressure triggers old habits, building coalitions before launching change, and remembering that leading from the top isn't about forcing motion, but about creating conditions where momentum spreads without you having to push every inch.

Structures Protect Themselves First

You can read a hundred leadership books and still miss this, because most of them skip the part where systems push back. Systems aren't neutral. Organizations reflexively guard their balance, often at the expense of momentum.

The terrain you're trying to lead through isn't just a collection of processes and people. It's an ecosystem built on tradeoffs: some intentional, some emergent, most invisible. And like any living system, it resists change because change threatens the balance that keeps everyone surviving, even if it's dysfunctional.

When David pushed for cross-functional scorecards, he wasn't just introducing a new reporting structure. He was poking the system's survival reflex. Every team had learned, over years of fire drills and shifting priorities, how to protect their credibility, their headcount, and their political leverage. Transparency wasn't neutral. It was a threat.

That's why people smiled in meetings but slow-walked initiatives afterward. It's why leaders agreed in principle but resisted in execution. They weren't lazy or malicious, they were obeying the deeper rules of the terrain: protect your turf, minimize risk, and survive the next reorg.

Coach's Commentary

Resistance isn't sabotage. It's the natural result of a landscape shaped by years of habit, not design. You're not here to bulldoze the terrain. You're here to study it, learn its contours, and chart a smarter path through it.

Once you see the terrain clearly, leading stops feeling like personal failure. You stop blaming yourself for every slowdown and stop taking every silent no as a sign you're not enough. You start navigating the real landscape strategically, not reactively, because structure isn't emotional, it's environmental. The leaders who thrive are the ones who learn to map the terrain, not moralize the resistance.

You Can't Brute-Force the Terrain

Work harder. That's the reflex. Longer hours, bigger decks, more 1-on-1s, extra check-ins. Push, polish, perfect, and hope sheer effort breaks through.

It doesn't.

You can't out-hustle a landscape designed to wear you down. You can only exhaust yourself trying to climb what you haven't mapped. David learned this the hard way.

Every time he tightened the timeline, someone pulled a resource. Every time he ran a faster meeting, someone rerouted the decision offline. Every time he clarified a priority, another project quietly got inflated to compete for attention. The more he pushed, the more the terrain pushed back. Not because people hated him or because they wanted him to fail, but because the system rewarded caution, not momentum. It protected what was familiar, because familiar felt safer than change.

You don't navigate dysfunction by muscling through it. You do it by reading the land. You need to spot the pressure points, the real levers, the well-worn trails that seem like shortcuts but loop you right back to the beginning. Because here's the shift that separates operators from architects: Leadership isn't about applying more force, it's about smarter footing. And smarter footing comes from seeing what's invisible to everyone else who's still grinding up the wrong hill.

The Four Zones of Terrain You Need to Map Before You Lead

You're not just leading inside a culture. You're moving through complex terrain, an unseen landscape shaped by priorities, processes, power structures, and people protecting themselves in ways they'll never admit in a meeting. If you want your leadership to stick, not stall, you need to map that terrain before you move.

Picture your proposal as a planned route on a topographical map. At the center? Your strategy. Your vision. The bold plan you're ready to lead. But this map is anything but blank. It's carved with elevation lines, hidden valleys, steep ridges, and winding passes. Ignore those contours, and you don't just risk slowing down, you risk stalling out completely.

There are four critical zones you need to read before you can navigate effectively. If you fail to see them, your best plans don't just stall, they die a slow, polite death. Let's walk the zones.

Zone 1: Power Flows and Decision Currents

This is the influence layer, the hidden contours of real authority. Forget the org chart, this zone is about who truly pulls the levers when pressure hits. Who slows things down without ever being blamed? Who gets quietly looped in at the last minute but holds real veto power? Who does the room wait for before making a move? And most importantly: Where do decisions actually get made? What conversations happen after the meeting that reshape what was just agreed to? If you don't map this zone, you're not strategizing, you're guessing.

Zone 2: Incentive Gradients

This is the reward terrain, the slope that quietly directs behavior. Not what leaders say they want, but what the system actually rewards. You don't get the behavior you ask for, you get the behavior you incentivize. Are heroics valued more than consistency? Do lone wolves rise faster than collaborators? Is short-term visibility prioritized over long-term value? If your proposal runs uphill against the real reward gradients, it's already sliding backward before it even starts.

Zone 3: Protection Zones

These are the ridges and choke points where leaders shield what's theirs. It's where momentum mysteriously dies.

Where do people say, "Not my lane?" Who gets defensive when visibility increases? Where does progress get delayed without a clear reason? These zones don't yield to force. You don't bulldoze them, you study them, design around them, or slowly and strategically disarm them.

Zone 4: System Storylines

This is the belief terrain, the mental maps people use to navigate the landscape. It's not what's printed on the walls, it's what gets whispered in the hallways and baked into daily choices. Every organization runs on unspoken stories. We might say, "Quality matters," but do we reward whoever ships first, not who ships best? We might say, "We innovate," but do we punish risk? We might say, "We trust people," but do we still double-approve everything? These storylines don't live in slides; they live in habits. If you don't reframe the story, you'll never reroute the system.

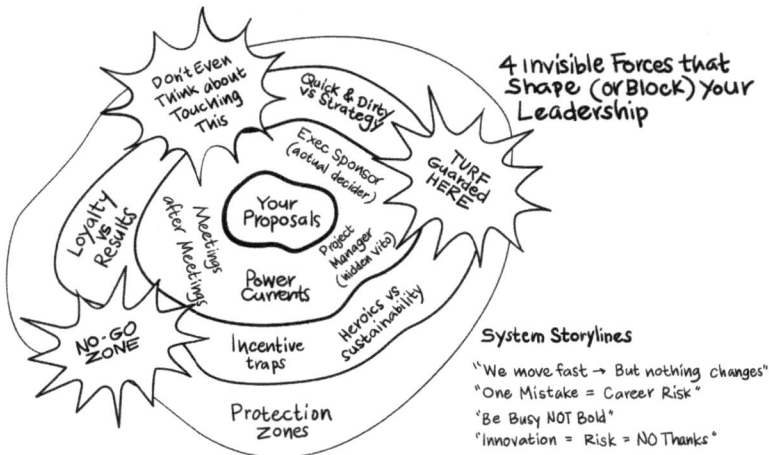

The Four Terrain Zones Leaders Miss

Wrap It Together

Those four zones, influence, incentives, protection, and story, are the real terrain your ideas must travel through. If you can't name them, you can't lead inside them, but once you see them clearly? Now you've got leverage.

Mapping Your Leverage Points

Once you see the landscape clearly, the question isn't: **"How do I fix everything?"**
It's: **"Where's the smartest point to push?"**
Strategic thinkers don't try to overhaul broken setups overnight. They find the smallest, highest-leverage moves that shift bigger patterns over time. When you map the system you're operating in, you want to look for three types of leverage points:

1. Structural Leverage

Where could a small change in a process, decision flow, or meeting rhythm free up massive energy downstream? For example: David didn't dismantle the entire reporting structure overnight. He started by quietly aligning key directors on shared success metrics before anything hit the official dashboards. That one alignment point lowered resistance by 30 percent and cracked open new momentum.

2. Relationship Leverage

Who are the connectors, the quiet influencers, the "hidden" leaders people listen to even when they don't have a big title? Systems move faster when you earn the trust of the real energy carriers, not just the ones who show up in formal stakeholder maps.

3. Story Leverage

What's the prevailing narrative the organization tells itself about how things work, and what new story could start shifting it? If the culture tells itself "risk gets punished," you're not going to win by shouting about innovation. You win by spotlighting and celebrating small, safe wins, rewiring the story through action, not slogans.

This is where leadership stops feeling like firefighting and starts feeling like real architecture. You're not chasing every spark; you're designing firebreaks. You're not trying to outmuscle resistance; you're finding the pivot points that move resistance without burning yourself out.

Why Structures Protect Themselves (and How to Move Anyway)

Every leadership terrain is shaped by an operating model that is designed, intentionally or not, to protect itself. When you introduce something new, you're not just bringing an idea. You're introducing a disruption to the terrain's fragile balance.

Most setups don't assess first; they defend. Change feels like a threat, even when it's right. Resistance doesn't mean your idea is bad. It just means the terrain is reacting the way it was shaped to and guarding what's familiar, even when what's familiar isn't working. That's what self-protecting environments do. They don't always push back directly. They just make your best ideas feel heavier than they should be.

Coach's Commentary

Systems rarely scream "No!" They whisper "Later," "Not yet," and "Not my problem" until your momentum starves itself.

When you understand that, you stop taking resistance personally. You stop trying to muscle through every obstacle. Instead, you start scanning the landscape for smart moves:

- Shrinking the risk.

- Building coalitions.

- Reframing the story.

- Finding one beachhead where the new idea can prove itself and spread.

You don't have to conquer the whole terrain in one move, you just have to outlast its reflex to shut you down. Naming the resistance doesn't make it vanish, but it makes it visible, and once it's visible, it's leadable.

Driving Question

What invisible terrain is shaping your leadership, and what moves are you making because of its contours, not in spite of them?

Your Coaching Question From Jim

If you stopped trying to fix everything today, and instead mapped the power lines, alliances, and hidden blockers around you, what truths would finally come into view?

Mini Challenge: System Scan + Pressure Points

Download Worksheet: W4 – System Scan Canvas

Let's stop reacting and start mapping the terrain. This week, carve out 30 minutes and sketch the system you're really inside, not the formal org chart, but the hidden topography of influence, power, and pressure.

Use these prompts to chart the landscape that's actually shaping your leadership.

Step 1: Map Your Landscape

Who are the key players around you? Not just decision-makers, think blockers, gatekeepers, quiet influencers, and shadow allies.

Step 2: Scan for Pressure

Next to each player, ask:

- What pressure are they under?
- What are they afraid of losing?
- What narrative are they protecting?

You're not judging. You're studying the terrain they operate in, so you can move through it with precision.

Step 3: Identify Two Pressure Points

These are the places where movement consistently gets stuck. Ask:

- Where does progress stall again and again?
- Who slows things down, even unintentionally?
- What's the silent risk no one wants to name?

Step 4: Design One Smart Move

Pick one pressure point and shift something. Not everything. Just one deliberate move. It could be:

- A pre-alignment conversation before the next decision meeting.
- A process tweak that clears static from the signal.
- A story shift that helps your team feel the "why" more clearly.

This is what system leaders do. They don't curse the map; they navigate smarter.

Final Reframe: Systems Don't Yield to Effort; They Yield to Strategy

You can't out-hustle a broken system, you can't out-grind a misaligned structure, and you definitely can't out-wait a culture that rewards staying small. Effort without awareness doesn't move the needle; it just moves you closer to burnout. Working harder isn't the flex. Redesigning the terrain so it works smarter? That's the move.

If you remember nothing else from this chapter, remember this:

You're not stuck because you're incapable. You're stuck because you're leading inside a terrain you haven't fully mapped. And if you can't map it, you can't move it.

Your job isn't to bulldoze through resistance. Your job is to study the terrain, find your footholds, and make the kind of moves that shift the whole system, without breaking yourself in the process. Because once you see the invisible landscape clearly, you're no longer stuck inside it. You're the one shaping it.

And now that you've read the current, mapped the terrain, and named the invisible forces, it's time to ask the bigger question: **What future are you actually building toward?**

We'll go there next.

CHAPTER 5

Redesign Your Role Before It Redesigns You

If your vision doesn't make your chest tighten a little,
it's not a vision, it's a corporate lullaby.

– Jim Saliba

You weren't hired for the job you're doing today. Not really. You were hired for a box, a neat little rectangle on an org chart, drawn by someone who was guessing what they needed, or who just needed a body in a seat.

Since then, your job hasn't stayed still. It grew. It morphed. It mutated into something heavier, messier, and harder to define. More meetings, more projects, and more "just one more thing" assignments nobody wrote down, but everyone expects you to juggle.

You know how it goes, you're not doing one job anymore. You're doing three while pretending it's one. That's why leadership doesn't feel like a simple promotion up the ladder. It feels like carrying a whole damn scaffolding system while smiling for the company photo.

So, if you won't define your role, no problem! Someone else will. They'll shape it around what's missing, what's politically convenient, and whatever mess they hope gets handled quietly so they don't have to. And if you let them, you'll wake up a year from now holding a job description you didn't choose, built from other people's emergencies, expectations, and shortcuts.

This chapter is about taking the pen back. It's about owning your role before it owns you, because if you don't define the role you're here to play, it will be defined **by default**, and leadership by default rarely ends the way you want it to.

Story: Tanya's Wake-Up Call About Her Real Role

You've met Tanya before, now it's time to watch her claim the role she was already carrying.

Tanya Brooks wasn't confused about her workload. As Acting COO, she knew she was carrying responsibilities that stretched far beyond her job description. She was running strategy sessions, coaching directors, cleaning up budget gaps, managing external partnerships, and holding cross-functional initiatives together with sheer willpower. But here's the catch: On paper, she was still "Acting." Temporary. Placeholder. Invisible scaffolding holding up a structure everyone relied on, but few ever acknowledged.

When we sat down for coaching, I asked her a simple question: **"What would happen if you stopped doing everything that isn't technically yours?"**

She blinked, paused for a moment, and laughed, but not the good kind. **"The place would fall apart,"** she said.

Exactly.

Tanya wasn't acting like a placeholder. She was already the architect, the stabilizer, the momentum engine. But because she hadn't named her true role or designed it with intention, she kept waiting for someone else to recognize what was already true. And the system? It was more than happy to let her carry the weight without adjusting the expectations, authority, or support to match.

That's when the work shifted. Instead of asking, "When will they notice?" Tanya started asking, "What does the role I'm already playing deserve to be designed like?"

Title aside, she sketched the actual shape of her impact. She mapped what she owned, what she influenced, what she was carrying that wasn't sustainable, and what needed to be formalized, delegated, or restructured if the business was going to grow without breaking her in the process.

She didn't just advocate for a title change. She started living into the CEO version of her role, not the helper version. Clearer boundaries. Sharper priorities. Visible ownership of strategic outcomes, not just execution details.

Six months later, the title caught up to her, but by then, it wasn't even the most important thing. Tanya didn't just redesign her role on paper. She redesigned how she occupied her seat at the table, with clarity, power, and undeniable ownership.

Tanya's Ladder Check

Tanya had been operating at Rung 3, the Fixer. High trust, high initiative, but still anchored in reaction and over-functioning. This shift marked her transition into Rung 5, the Architect. She stopped plugging every hole and started shaping the structure itself, not by waiting for permission, but by naming her role, aligning it to the outcomes that mattered, and showing up like the leader the business already needed her to be.

The Lie About Job Descriptions

You've got a title, a job description, and a dotted-line org chart. None of them tell the real story of what you lead or what's on your shoulders. Maybe it was half-true when you first took the role. Maybe you were doing what the bullet points said for about three months. Then reality set in. Reorgs hit, fire drills took over, and new executives stepped in. Suddenly, you weren't doing the job you were hired for; you were doing the job the unspoken rules demanded.

Tanya Brooks knew this pain intimately. Officially, she was the Acting COO, covering for a leadership gap while the CEO decided whether to do a search. Unofficially, she was running ops, coaching directors, battling budget chaos, putting out customer fires, and shielding the team from random drive-by "priorities" thrown in from above. The job she had on paper didn't match the job she lived every day. And every time she tried to find her footing, the ground shifted.

It took a brutal conversation, one where Tanya admitted she felt like she was "holding it all together but still somehow failing," to see it clearly. She wasn't failing. She was leading a role that had never been formally defined. That's more common than most execs admit.

Coach's Commentary

Job descriptions expire the day real pressure hits. Savvy execs stop clinging to what they were handed and start designing what's actually needed.

Your Current Role Was Built by Accident

Most roles weren't designed intentionally. They evolved through shortcuts, compromises, emergency band-aids, and "just for now" decisions that somehow never got revisited. Somewhere between the original job posting and today's daily chaos, your role became a Frankenstein's monster. A little bit of your predecessor's leftovers. A little bit of the last reorg's unfinished business. A lot of "someone has to do it" work that got dumped in your lap because you were competent enough not to drop it.

The result? You're operating from a job description nobody ever wrote down, but everybody expects you to fulfill. And every time you say yes to filling those invisible gaps, you harden them into concrete. You're not just doing the job. You're defining it. And if you're not careful, you'll be defining it by accident, not design.

The Hidden Creep of Responsibility

You didn't sign up for chaos. You didn't ask for three people's jobs folded into yours. And you sure as hell didn't request the meetings, projects, and silent expectations that piled up one slow layer at a time. But here you are, stuck running a role that bears little resemblance to the one you were hired for.

This is one of the most common pitfalls I see: the slow expansion of responsibility without the matching clarity, authority, or support. Nobody calls it out because it doesn't happen all at once. It's not a bold announcement. It's a slow, quiet evolution.

You're good at fixing fires, so more fires come your way. You're reliable under pressure, so more pressure gets routed to you. You're the one who "can handle it," so handling becomes your brand. And because you're competent, you absorb it. Because you're proud of your craft, you shoulder it. Because you want to protect your team, your clients, and your work, you wear it. Until one day you wake up and realize you're leading an unacknowledged empire of problems that were never supposed to be yours, and no one even notices you're carrying them.

Coach's Commentary

If you don't design the shape of your role, your environment will design it for you, and it will design it for its own survival, not your success.

Redesign Your Role: Start With the Responsibility Audit

You can't lead what you haven't named, and you definitely can't own a role that's been Frankensteined together by a hundred invisible forces.

Look at the following Venn diagram with its three overlapping circles labeled "Assigned," "Assumed," and "Inherited." In the center, where all three overlap, is the burden leaders often carry without clear authority or acknowledgment. "Assigned" covers formal responsibilities, "Assumed" reflects the work you picked up because no one else did, and "Inherited" includes legacy tasks that were never reassigned but somehow became yours. This visual helps leaders sort and name what they're really carrying, and what might need to be redefined, delegated, or shed. That's why your first move isn't just "stepping up" into your leadership. It's stepping back and auditing what you're truly carrying.

YOUR FRANKENSTEIN ROLE

A job description you didn't sign up for — but ended up owning.

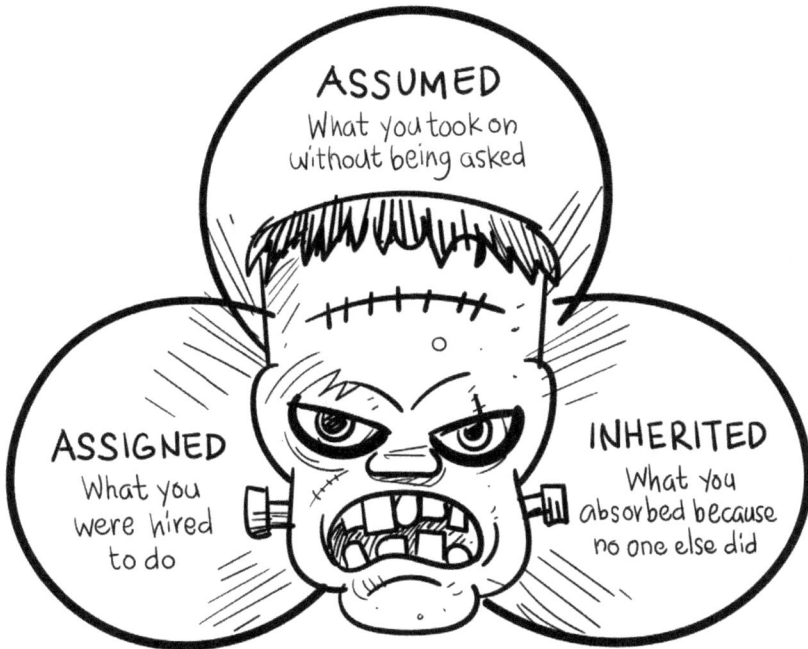

ASSUMED
What you took on without being asked

ASSIGNED
What you were hired to do

INHERITED
What you absorbed because no one else did

When I coach executives through this process, there's one thing I always point out upfront: Your current role is a swamp of **assigned**, **assumed**, and quietly **inherited** responsibilities. Some you signed up for. Some were handed to you. Some you picked up because no one else did, and now they're welded to your identity, whether you like it or not.

If you don't name them, they own you. So, here's the Responsibility Audit framework: three brutal questions you need to sit with before you redesign anything.

1. What Have I Officially Been Assigned?

This is the easy part: your formal job description, your goals, your metrics, your KPIs. If you actually have a clean, current job description that matches your real life, you're in the 1%. Frame it. Otherwise, start by documenting what's been explicitly assigned to you:

- Teams you manage
- Projects you own
- Metrics you're held accountable for
- Initiatives you're responsible for launching, leading, or delivering

You need this baseline because clarity isn't optional, it's leadership oxygen.

2. What Responsibilities Have I Silently Assumed?

This is the messy part, the work you've taken on without formal ownership because:

- You care
- You're competent
- Other people dropped the ball, and you couldn't watch it roll off the table
- Someone asked nicely (and you didn't know how to say no)

Write it all down. Every recurring fire you're quietly putting out. Every side project you "volunteered" for but never let go of. Every informal leadership function, mentoring, fixing broken workflows, smoothing cross-team drama, that's somehow become "your thing." Because the stuff you never signed up for? That's usually what's bleeding you dry. You're carrying weight that no one else sees, values, or protects.

3. What Responsibilities Have I Accidentally Inherited?

This is the hidden burden, the stuff you never agreed to, but that stuck to you anyway. Inherited messes come from:

- A previous leader who bailed without finishing their handoffs

- A reorg that shifted "temporary" projects onto your plate

- Cultural gaps where nobody ever named a clear owner, so guess who got volunteered?

These inherited responsibilities distort your credibility quietly. Because they eat your time, hijack your priorities, and make it look like you're scattered or slow, even when you're drowning trying to keep things alive that should have been sunset three years ago. Audit the swamp first, then start building the real map.

Leadership Challenge Anchor: Step 3—Storyboard Your Future (Part 1)

The Six-Step Leadership Challenge started with the mirror (introspection) and the map (extrospection). Now we're going to pivot. Step 3 is about moving from survival into design, starting with the role you're meant to lead.

This chapter is part one of that design phase. Before you can create a vision for what's next, you have to define the seat you're truly sitting in now. The next chapter builds on this because once you see your real role clearly, the next move is to define where that role is going.

Redefine the Role You're Actually Meant to Lead

It's time to stop playing janitor for a job description that doesn't exist anymore. They don't stay static. Step into any leadership role, and it'll start mutating before your second coffee. The paper version you signed up for was just the starting point. What you're really leading now is something far bigger and far less defined: people, systems, projects, fires, gaps. That's the real job, and if you keep measuring yourself against the old blueprint, you'll stay locked in survival mode instead of designing an executive platform that fits the job you're actually doing.

Your real role isn't about carrying every leftover task your predecessors abandoned. It's about stepping back, surveying the ground, and asking:

- What am I really responsible for, whether it was handed to me or not?

- What critical outcomes truly rely on my leadership, not just my execution?

- Where is the true edge of my domain, the one I'm expected to own even if nobody spelled it out?

If you don't redefine your role, someone else will, and most of the time, they'll define it based on what makes their life easier, not what grows your leadership or your impact.

You don't owe anyone the outdated shape they thought you'd squeeze into. You owe yourself (and your people) a clear, strategic, intentional version of the role that reflects the terrain you're leading today.

Tanya's Role Was Evolving, But Her Framing Hadn't Caught Up

By now, you've seen Tanya Brooks grow from a stabilizing force to a strategic driver. As Acting COO of a fast-scaling tech and manufacturing firm, she had long since outgrown her original brief: "Keep operations humming while we scale."

What she was really doing was setting strategy, shaping priorities, and making executive tradeoffs that determined where the business invested and where it pulled back. But when Tanya introduced herself, she still said things like "keeping the trains running." She was operating at executive altitude, but framing her value like an operator. So people treated her accordingly.

They handed her projects without a strategy, expected her to say yes to everything, and saw her as the fixer of broken processes, not the architect of where the company was heading. Because Tanya hadn't explicitly redefined her role, hadn't named the shift, and claimed the altitude, the system kept pulling her back to the one she had already outgrown.

That's the slow slide. If you don't redefine your role, the system around you will define it for you. Usually by default, and usually smaller than you deserve.

The Blueprint Shift: From Job Description to Leadership Mandate

Here's the shift that separates bold thinkers from stuck operators:

1.   Stop leading to your job description.

2.   Start leading to your leadership mandate.

Your **job description** is a static document built for yesterday's needs. Your **leadership mandate** is the living design of what your area, and your organization, needs to thrive tomorrow. You don't redesign your role by updating your LinkedIn profile. You redesign it by building a new blueprint, one that acknowledges the invisible work you're already doing, the ownership you're already carrying, and the strategic weight you're already moving.

That blueprint starts with three hard questions:

1.   What outcomes am I already responsible for, whether they're named or not?

2.   Where does my leadership make the biggest difference, whether it's formally recognized or not?

3. What new outcomes should I be aiming for if I want to build a leadership footprint that lasts longer than my next quarterly review?

Because if you're still leading like your job is to hit last year's KPIs when you're now responsible for shifting next year's strategy, you're not just playing small, you're endangering your future. You're telling the system to keep you boxed in, even when you have the keys to something bigger.

Build Your Ownership Blueprint

You're not just redesigning tasks, you're redesigning ownership. The fastest way to make leadership visible, scalable, and durable is to claim clear ownership of what actually matters and let the noise fall away. But you can't just "try harder" at your existing calendar. You need a blueprint: a simple, brutal map of what's truly yours to own, shape, and drive forward.

That's what the **Ownership Blueprint Canvas** is built for, and it's part of your Mini Challenge Worksheet for this chapter. Here's what you'll map:

- **Your Primary Zone.** What is the beating heart of the space you're responsible for? Not the nice-to-have projects. The critical systems, outcomes, relationships, and levers.

- **The Critical Few.** What three to five strategic responsibilities or initiatives define success in your role? Not your whole calendar. The ones that actually move the mission forward.

- **The Influence Web.** Who are the stakeholders, partners, and teams you must align, amplify, or unlock to succeed?

- **The Landmines.** Where are the hidden friction points, inherited messes, or political tripwires you need to navigate carefully, or redesign completely?

- **Your New Role Title.** If you had to rename your role to match what you really do (not what's on your business card), what would you call it?

This isn't corporate vision-boarding; this is executive design. Because if you can't name what you own, you can't grow it, and if you don't name what you're **not** going to own, you'll keep drowning in everyone else's priorities.

Reminder: You'll grab the full **Ownership Blueprint Canvas** inside your Mini Challenge Worksheet at the end of this chapter.

Ownership Blueprint Canvass

Primary Zone
What's the core space you're responsible for?

The Critical Few	Influence Web	Landmines
What 3-5 outcomes or responsibilities define success in your role?	Who do you need to align, activate, or unlock?	Where are the invisible tripwires or inherited messes?

Redesign Notes
What do you need to shed, hand back, or delegate?

Role Rename
If you renamed your role to reflect what you actually do, what would it be?

Not later. Not someday. Now. Because redesigning your role isn't a "nice to have." It's how you stop being the default operator and start being the architect of your area.

Coach's Commentary

Leadership isn't about doing more; it's about claiming more with clarity. The clearer you are about what you own, the clearer everyone else gets, too.

Vague roles create chaos, but clear ownership creates authority. When you build your blueprint, you don't just manage work, you design momentum.

Driving Question

☞ What parts of my current role are by design, and what parts have I just been absorbing without clarity or intent?

Your Coaching Question From Jim

☞ If you were hired tomorrow *only* to own your space at the highest level, what work, meetings, tasks, or patterns would you immediately stop doing (or hand back)?

Mini Challenge: Define Your Ownership Blueprint

✎ Download Worksheet: W5 – Ownership Blueprint Canvas

Step 1: Do a raw audit.

What are all the teams, projects, outcomes, decisions, and relationships you currently touch, shape, or influence?

Step 2: Split them.

- *Real Ownership*: Responsibilities that align with your highest impact.

- *Accidental Absorption*: Stuff you picked up because no one else did, or because the system rewarded it.

Step 3: Redesign—Draft a one-page Ownership Blueprint.

- What you truly own.

- What you influence.

- What you need to shed, hand back, or redesign.

Step 4: Bonus Move—Draft a sample ownership narrative (your leadership value prop).

"If someone asked me what I own here, I could say: *I lead X by driving Y outcomes with Z impact.*" (Keep it real, simple, and powerful.)

Final Reframe: Leadership Grows From Clarity, Not Accumulation

If you remember nothing else from this chapter, remember this:

You don't grow by carrying more. You grow by owning sharper.

Leadership without boundaries isn't leadership, it's exhaustion. You're not here to be a glorified project manager, a heroic firefighter, or an invisible fixer. You're here to steer the direction by design, not by default, and that design starts by claiming the true shape of your role, before anyone else defines it for you. Because once you own the role you were meant to lead, you create the foundation for a vision that's actually worth building toward.

And that's exactly where we're headed next: Not just understanding the space you already lead, but designing the future you're ready to claim.

CHAPTER 6

Design the Future That Pulls You Forward

Don't build a vision that fits where you are.
Build one that scares you into moving.

– Jim Saliba

You're not lost.

You're just moving fast without a clear destination, and wondering why it still feels like treading water. When you ask someone to describe their vision, you'll often get a two-line answer that sounds ambitious, but could belong to any company, any team, anywhere. Phrases like "We want to be best-in-class," or "We drive innovation," or "We empower teams to deliver value." On the surface, they sound impressive, but if you listen closely, they're placeholders. Vague aspirations dressed up as strategy. They check a box, but they don't move anyone forward.

That's not a vision. That's a slogan with a marketing budget.

Coach's Commentary

Most leaders don't realize how much energy they waste chasing better execution inside broken stories. If your vision sounds impressive but feels hollow, don't decorate it. Rebuild it

Vision doesn't fit on a poster. It's not a generic statement you could slap on a thousand conference banners. It's a story, a vivid, lived-in snapshot of the future you're building. It's something you can see, feel, and fight for, and if you don't name that future, you'll be stuck repeating the present. You'll get better at putting out fires. You'll become more efficient at managing chaos. You'll optimize a broken system instead of replacing it. You'll run faster in the same circle. Meanwhile, your team will stay busy, but not bold, engaged, but not energized, and delivering, but not elevated.

This is where Step 3 sharpens.

In Chapter 5, you reclaimed the real shape of your role. Now it's time to name the future it's meant to lead.

This is still Step 3 of the Six-Step Leadership Challenge: **Storyboard your future.**

I'm not talking about a vague slogan, but a clear, strategic picture of what life, leadership, and progress look like when your role fully aligns with your values, your strengths, and the outcomes that matter most. And it starts with more than ambition; it starts with vision. Not a polished version of your current job, but a future bold enough to demand a new level of leadership from you. One that pulls you forward.

Because vague plans push. Real direction pulls.

The Vision Vacuum

Michael had already made serious strides. He'd started stepping back from the grind of daily execution. He was coaching more, protecting strategic time, and saying "no" to tasks that didn't align with his new role. But something still wasn't clicking.

"Even with all this clarity," he said one afternoon, "I still don't know what I'm aiming for."

You can fix your calendar. You can sharpen your ownership. You can clean up your role. But without a clear future in sight, all you've done is make the current system run smoother.

We zoomed out. I asked him: "Let's say you've got the headcount, the budget, the buy-in. The friction's gone. The roadblocks are cleared. Now show me: What does a week in your world look like when it's actually working?"

Not someday perfect. Not flawless. Just focused. Just a bold, clear version of how leadership feels, sounds, and moves when it's aligned with what you're really trying to build. He paused, and then, slowly, the real picture started to emerge:

"My mornings don't start with firefighting anymore. They start at the whiteboard, not the inbox. I'm coaching my directors through real plays, launching cross-functional pilots, tackling systemic blockers, and making bets that matter. No more chasing updates, no more holding hands.

By afternoon, I'm in the future. Scouting partnerships, designing the next move, thinking five steps ahead instead of being stuck two steps behind. I'm not in every decision, but the right ones still find me. My team moves with confidence, without needing constant signoff. Slack isn't blowing up with chaos, it's full of wins, momentum, and shoutouts.

By Friday, I still have energy. I'm not dragging myself home, tapped out and checked out. I've got fuel in the tank, enough to be present with my family, to plan a weekend we'll actually enjoy, and to live the life I'm building.

I'm not the safety net anymore. I'm the multiplier.

Coach's Commentary

Leadership gravity comes from knowing what future you're protecting, not how many tasks you can juggle. You're not building speed, you're building pull

And in that moment, everything shifted. His decisions got faster, his delegation got sharper, and his boundaries got clearer and non-negotiable because now he wasn't just managing tasks. He was protecting something real. A future he could see. A life he actually wanted. One that deserved his best leadership, not just his best effort.

Here's the bigger pattern: Almost every executive I've coached, across industries, levels, and roles, hits the same wall at some point. When I ask them to imagine their leadership life 12 to 18 months from now, the first reaction is almost always the same: "Gee, I don't know." It's not because they lack ambition. It's because they've been moving so fast for so long, reacting for so many cycles, that they've stopped asking the question altogether. But when you slow them down, when you give them even a little space to think, something else emerges, and it's surprisingly consistent.

They start to say things like:

- "My calendar would be more strategic and less operational."

- "I wouldn't be firefighting every day."

- "My team would own their work instead of throwing it back on my plate."

It's not that they don't know what they want. It's that they haven't given themselves permission to name it. And once they do? Everything changes. They stop working just to survive the week. They start working to protect the future they actually want to live in.

Your North Star isn't invented, it's uncovered, and then you choose to defend it.

The Future You Design Shouldn't Hang on a Wall, It Should Pull You In

In a world where everything shifts weekly, markets, strategies, org charts, it's tempting to wonder if vision work is even worth it. Why bother painting a picture of the future when the ground keeps moving underneath you? But when everything is changing, a strong vision isn't a luxury. It's a lifeline.

Clarity isn't about slogans or posters. It's not a tagline you announce once at an all-hands meeting. It's something you feel. It's the magnet that pulls your decisions forward when the path gets messy. It's the anchor that keeps your leadership from getting swept away in reactionary chaos.

It's personal.

The best leaders I coach don't just have vision statements for their companies. They have painted storylines for their roles, their teams, their products, even their own growth. They can describe what success actually looks and feels like, not just in spreadsheets, but in real life. They say things like:

- "My team runs with confidence when I'm out of the office."

- "We launch work that makes customers send thank-you notes."

- "My calendar reflects my highest value, not just my availability."

- "I feel proud of the impact I've had, because it's the impact I chose."

These aren't corporate objectives. They're personal leadership stories, and they change everything. Because when you write a future you actually want to live in, you don't just survive change, you lead through it. You stop reacting to chaos and start authoring your path. That's the difference between a good manager and a transformational leader. One adapts to the noise. The other builds the music.

The Hidden Risk of a Small Vision

There's a danger that rarely gets named: **If your vision is too small, it doesn't protect you; it shrinks you.**

A small vision convinces you that you're making progress when all you're really doing is maintaining. You get better at hitting deliverables, but not better at changing the game. You keep teams in motion, but you're not moving them anywhere new. You become excellent, but invisible. And over time, something worse happens: You stop seeing yourself as someone capable of more.

A safe vision feels good today, but it costs you tomorrow. Every time you choose a vision that's cautious instead of compelling, you're not just limiting your growth; you're anchoring yourself to the lower rungs of impact, because when your future is vague, your leadership stays reactive. You solve problems, but you don't unlock potential. You manage the work, but you don't mobilize people. You keep things afloat but never raise the tide.

This is how leaders get stuck. Not from lack of skill, but from lack of stretch. Not from failure, but from playing too small. Without a bold destination, you don't rise, you swirl. You end up rewriting your story into something quieter, safer, easier to replace.

That's why your vision has to stretch you. It has to make you a little uncomfortable. It shouldn't make you reckless, and it shouldn't be a fantasy, but it must be bold enough that the version of you today can't fully deliver it without stepping up to become something stronger.

If your vision doesn't make you nervous at least once while writing it, it's not a vision. It's a maintenance plan. And maintenance doesn't build momentum. It doesn't build legacy. And it doesn't build the kind of leadership story you came here to write.

Let's anchor this moment inside the bigger journey, the Six-Step Leadership Challenge. In Steps 1 and 2, you laid the foundation.

- **Step 1: Look inward.** You named the hidden fears and reflexes that quietly run your leadership when pressure hits.

- **Step 2: Look around.** You mapped the cultural currents and structural terrain shaping how things move, or stall, around you.

Now you're inside **Step 3: Storyboard your future.** This is where ownership starts to get real.

In the last chapter, you redefined the role you're truly here to play. Now, in Chapter 6, we take the next leap: You define what that role is meant to build. Not a slogan. Not a tidy vision statement. A real, tangible future worth protecting. Because here's the turning point: Until now, you've been managing what's in front of you. But leadership that lasts, the kind that actually changes things, isn't about managing. It's about creating. And you can't create what you haven't envisioned.

This is the hinge in your leadership journey. It's where your job stops being about execution and starts being about direction. It's where your team stops watching your output and starts responding to your clarity. It's where your calendar, your choices, and your energy all become aligned with something that actually matters.

You don't just lead the present. You lead the future. And if you don't define that future, you can't protect it. You'll keep bending for the urgent, instead of building for the important. Vision isn't a luxury; it's your anchor, because without a clear future in sight, you're not leading, you're just reacting.

Vision gets talked about more than it gets built. You've seen it: The slick one-liner in the company deck. The "North Star" that shifts with every reorg. The bold-sounding paragraph that doesn't drive a single decision. It's no wonder leaders tune it out. They've lived through the buzzwords. They've watched executives change the narrative every quarter. They've seen "alignment sessions" that change nothing but slide formatting.

So they double down on what feels solid: KPI dashboards. Quarterly plans. Organizational charts. But those are management tools, not vision, and without a real vision to guide them, those tools become directionless. You don't get momentum, you get motion sickness. You stay busy, but you stop moving toward something that actually matters.

David's Stalled Strategy

By now, you know David Chen, smart, strategic, system-minded CTO. He'd already leveled up his role, delegated more, mapped the terrain, and started leading from altitude. So, when his new transformation initiative stalled, he didn't default to blame. He came to our next session frustrated, but reflective.

"I know the structure makes sense," he said. "I've laid it out, simplified the handoffs, and cleared the friction, but people aren't moving. They're nodding, then hesitating."

We looked closer. And what we found wasn't a flaw in the plan. It was a missing picture.

David had mapped deliverables, not desirables. The team didn't have a reason to care. They couldn't see the destination—what this change would feel like, look like, or mean for them once it worked. So, he rewrote the story. Not the technical narrative. The vision.

He described the kind of culture it would enable, the clarity it would bring, and the speed and confidence it would unlock for teams across the org. That's when things clicked. People saw themselves in the future. Energy returned. Alignment rose.

David didn't need a new plan, he needed a visible future his team could believe in. He stopped transmitting strategy and started sharing vision.

Tanya's Next-Level Shift

I saw the opposite challenge with Tanya Brooks. Where David lacked clarity on the vision, Tanya had the tools, the trust, and a green light to think bigger. But she kept solving for short-term wins. She kept playing safe. She kept operating two levels below where she needed to be.

Not because she lacked ambition. Tanya had plenty. But she didn't have the picture. She hadn't taken the time to define what "bigger" actually looked like, not just for the company, but for herself as a leader. Her calendar was full, her meetings were sharp, but her energy? It was fragmented. She was advancing execution without anchoring it to a future she could name.

When we stepped back and sketched her vision story, twelve to eighteen months out, everything changed. We didn't just whip up a mission statement. By the end of that session, Tanya had a vivid map of her leadership life: What she owned, what she delegated, what made her proud, and what made her unstoppable.

From that moment on, her posture shifted. Her decisions came faster. Her voice got louder. Her influence grew without chasing it.

Tanya didn't need more responsibilities. She needed a destination.

Coach's Commentary

A clear vision isn't just a leadership tool. It's a ladder upgrade.

Tanya was operating at Rung 3 fixing problems, building trust, and holding the center, but once she named her vision, she started leading from Rung 5. She wasn't just reacting, she was designing. She wasn't waiting to be seen, she was shaping what came next.

That's the shift that vision makes possible. It doesn't just give you direction. It redefines how others experience your leadership and how you experience yourself.

Let's Build One, Together

Right now, stop thinking like a manager and start thinking like an architect. You're not just optimizing your week; you're designing the leadership life you're ready to own.

We're stepping into **Step 3 (Part 2):** Define the future your role is meant to build, the one bold enough to guide your energy, earn your protection, and pull others with you.

This is where everything converges. You've claimed your leadership, decoded the environment, and redesigned the role you're truly meant to lead, but vision doesn't live inside any one of those pieces alone. It only becomes clear when you hold them together, your ownership, your terrain, and your role, in service of something bigger.

Now we build that something. A future that's not just aspirational, but actionable. Not vague ambition, but a clear direction, one that reshapes how you lead, decide, and design what comes next. Your vision isn't built in a vacuum. It grows from your clarity and your context. The better you understand yourself, and the system you're operating in, the sharper your vision will become.

So, let's get practical. I want you to imagine your leadership life one year from now. Not your company's press release goals. Not your department's next OKR cycle.

Your life. Your team. Your outcomes.

Where are you? What are you working on? What fills your calendar, and what never even touches it? How does your team operate without you in the room? What are people saying about your leadership when you're not in the meeting? What impact are you most proud of?

Write it like it's already happening. Write it like the budget's been approved, the politics cleared, the blockers handled. Write it boldly enough that you'd feel jealous if someone else described it as their real life.

BUILDING A COMPELLING VISION

AMBITION	TENSION	ELEVATION	VIVID STORYLINE	PULL TEST
What do I want to build?	What am I sick of tolerating?	What would feel bold, proud, and energizing?	What does a week look like when this works?	Would I feel, jealous if someone else lived this?

So, how do you actually build a compelling leadership vision?

You start with five simple prompts, questions designed to crack open clarity, unlock momentum, and make the future feel personal, not abstract.

Ambition: *What do I want to build?* Forget your job description. What's the bigger outcome you actually care about creating?

Tension: *What am I sick of tolerating?* Frustration is a clue. It points to the cracks. The stuff you know needs to change.

Elevation: *What would feel bold, proud, and energizing?* Don't build from fear. Build from pride. What version of leadership would make you stand taller?

Vivid Storyline: *What does a week look like when this works?* Zoom in. Paint it in color. Where are you, what are you doing, and what's changed?

Pull Test: *Would I feel jealous if someone else lived this?* That's your gut check. If it doesn't feel magnetic, it's not your vision yet.

This is your blueprint. Now let's put some skin on it. Here's what a vivid vision sounds like:

- "I walk into our Monday huddle, and before I even speak, the conversation's already crackling. My team owns the priorities, pushes the edge, and I'm there to calibrate, not to steer. They don't wait for my lead, they run with it."

- "Three mornings a week, I pour my focus into the next wave of leaders who are sharp, hungry, and already pushing past where I was at their stage. This isn't just development. It's legacy-building, and the most energizing part of my calendar."

- "Our product drops don't just meet targets, they bend the market. Customers light up, and competitors scramble. We're not reacting to trends, we're defining them."

- "When the CEO and CFO call the strategy meeting, I'm not invited for formality. I'm invited first because when the stakes are high, they want my clarity in the room before anything gets decided."

This isn't daydreaming. This is blueprinting. You aren't building fantasy. You're building the future you're going to lead into existence.

The Future-State Filter: How to Know If You're Aiming High Enough

When you finish writing your vision story, test it against this quick rubric:

Question	If YES	If NO
Does it make you a little nervous?	Good. Growth lives here.	Push further. You're playing it too safe.
Can you vividly picture it like a movie scene?	Good. It's specific enough to be real.	Too vague. Flesh it out until you *feel* it.
Would future-you be proud to live in it?	Good. It's aligned with your bigger leadership.	Recalibrate. You're settling for "better," not "transformational."
Is it bigger than what you know exactly how to achieve today?	Good. You'll have to stretch and evolve.	Expand. If you can fully map it today, it's a to-do list, not a vision.
Does it align with who you are becoming, not just who you are now?	Good. Vision pulls you forward.	Refine. You're designing for today's comfort, not tomorrow's growth.

Final Test: When you read your vision out loud, does your chest tighten a little with excitement *and* a little fear? If yes, you're ready. If not, rewrite it until it feels alive.

Want to Go Deeper? Try the Postcard From the Future.

Before you move forward, anchor your vision with a short leadership experiment. Write a message from your future self to your present self. Imagine the vision you just described is already real. What would future-you thank you for? What decision would you be most proud you made? What reminder would you send back across time so you don't lose the thread?

It doesn't need to be long. A few lines can carry enormous weight. For example:

"Thank you for protecting the vision when convenience tried to compromise it. Thank you for holding your altitude when urgency begged you to drop. This team, this momentum, this future, they exist because you chose to lead at full height, even when it was lonely and no one was clapping yet.

You didn't just chase outcomes.

You built a reality no one else could see, until you made it undeniable."

This isn't planning. This is conviction. And conviction moves mountains.

Driving Question

- What does your leadership life look like twelve months from now, if everything clicks? Not what you hope. Not what you tolerate. What you actually live.

Your Coaching Question From Jim

- If you had to live inside your vision story tomorrow, what would you need to change today to make it possible?

Mini Challenge: The Vision Story Canvas

✎ Download Worksheet: W6 – Vision Story Canvas

Block 30 minutes this week. Not to think. Not to plan. To build.

Write a vivid, specific story of your leadership life twelve to eighteen months from today, as if it's already real. Anchor three key snapshots:

- **Your Role.** What fills your calendar? What work demands your best energy?

- **Your Team.** How do they operate without you? What are they achieving because of how you lead?

- **Your Impact.** How is your leadership changing outcomes, and how are others describing you when you're not in the room?

Don't write what's safe. Write what you actually want to live. If your story feels comfortable, stretch it bigger. If it feels practical, push it toward bold. If it doesn't make your chest tighten slightly with excitement or fear, you're not done yet.

When you finish, read it out loud. Feel it. Then ask yourself: **What single shift could you make this week to move one step closer to that story becoming real?**

Not someday or eventually. This week.

Final Reframe: Strategy Follows Direction

You've done more than claim your area. You've done more than clean up your calendar or fix your role. You've defined what's next. And that future isn't a wish list. It's a direction. A decision. A design you can start protecting and building, starting now. Because when the pressure hits, and it will, you don't need more rules. You don't need more tools. You need a reason to hold your ground.

Purpose holds the line.

Your future direction keeps you moving when the shortcuts look tempting. A strong sense of direction sharpens your decisions when priorities start to blur. Your strategic direction gives your leadership durability, not just when things are going well, but when they aren't.

You don't rise to your goals; you rise to your vision, and if you don't write the future you want, someone else will write it for you. You want to Lead Like a CEO? Then act like the architect of what comes next, because your team isn't just following your instructions. They're following your clarity.

Write your future like it matters, because it does. Lead like it's already real, because it's waiting for you.

If you remember nothing else from this chapter, remember this:

Leadership without a future in mind isn't leadership. It's maintenance in disguise.

In the next chapters, we'll move from design to execution. You'll learn how to turn this vision into a living system with clear behaviors, experiments, and practices that make it visible, durable, and real. Because vision without action is fantasy. Action turns clarity into power so you can start shaping what comes next

Let's get to work.

CHAPTER 7

Start Bold. Think Small. Move Fast.

*The fastest way to change your leadership
story is to stop telling the old one.*

– Jim Saliba

You don't need a five-year plan.

You need a first step. Not a vision board. Not a soul-searching sabbatical. A single step. You don't need a new promotion, or a new title, or a new team. You need to start acting like the strategic force you already are, just slightly louder. Everyone loves strategy until it gets sweaty.

This chapter is where you stop hand-waving strategy and start *building* it for real. One action. One decision. One breath of boldness that puts you in motion.

Why I Keep Talking About Experiments

You've heard me use the word *experiment* more than a few times already in this book. That's not an accident. When I say *experiment,* I don't just mean *try something.* I mean something much more specific and much more powerful.

An experiment isn't just action. It's intentional learning. It's leadership in test mode. And here's why that matters: I often see leaders who don't fail for lack of effort, but from overcommitting to big plans without enough learning along the way.

That's where experiments come in.

Think back to your fifth-grade science fair. You didn't need a corporate budget or a polished deck. You needed six things:

1. **A Clear Question.** What are you trying to learn or shift?

2. **A Hypothesis.** What do you think will happen, and why?

3. **A Simple Plan.** What specific action will you take?

4. **A Time Frame.** Short, fast, focused. 30 days or less.

5. **A Way to Measure.** What data, behavior, or signal will you track?

6. **A Reflection.** What happened? What surprised you? What's your next move?

That's an experiment, and it's the backbone of how we build traction here. Not perfect plans, endless meetings, or reactive firefighting. Just small, strategic tests that turn insight into motion, and motion into momentum.

So, if you've been wondering why this book doesn't hand you a templated roadmap, now you know. Because leadership doesn't need more templates, it needs more learning loops, and experiments are how we build them.

The Story: Why First Steps Matter More Than Perfect Plans

I've never really been a runner. I'm a cyclist by nature. Give me smooth pedaling and a long ride, and I'm in my element. Years ago, just to check a box, I ran a marathon. It wasn't my Zen. It wasn't natural to me. But I finished it.

More recently, my daughter got into running, and she invited me to join her. We've now done a few events together, and we're signed up for another: the Detroit International Half Marathon. I'm not doing it because I love running. I'm doing it because I love moving forward with her.

And every race, every training run, starts the same way: One step, then the next, and then the next. You don't get halfway through a race by strategizing the perfect pace chart. You get there by starting.

Leadership experiments work the same way. They're not about executing a flawless blueprint. They're about committing to movement and letting motion sharpen the plan. And right now, it's time to move.

Setting the Stage: Step 4 of the Six-Step Leadership Challenge

You've already done the foundational work:

- You claimed your leadership, not just the title, but the territory.
- You decoded the terrain, culture, system, politics, all of it.
- You named the future you're here to build.

Now it's time to stop sketching the map and start walking it.

This is Step 4 of the Six-Step Leadership Challenge: **Design your plan.**

Not with a deck. Not with a wish list. With motion. Small, strategic, testable action that moves your story forward, one bold experiment at a time.

Framing the Next Four Chapters

In these next four chapters, you're not building just any leadership plan; you're building a living operating system of leadership test runs. No experiment is random. Each one is designed to move you forward right now, based on where you are today.

Your first experiments will be different from the ones you run 90 days from now, one year from now, even five years down the line, because leadership isn't static, and neither is your growth. What feels bold today will feel basic tomorrow, if you're doing it right.

These Chapters 7, 8, 9, and 10 are where we plant the seeds: small, strategic moves that create traction, clarity, and momentum. Later, in Chapters 11 and 12, we'll focus on executing and adjusting those experiments through fast learning loops. And in Chapters 13 and 14, we'll show you how to scale your initiatives into the 90-Day Ascent Loop and accelerate your impact at scale. But it all starts here: One step. One trial. One defining moment.

Welcome to Step 4: Action Strategy

Up until now, most of your energy has been spent reshaping how you see yourself and how you see the system you're operating in.

- You've learned to claim your area.

- You've learned to map the hidden forces around you.

- You've named the future you want to build.

Now it's time to build the bridge from vision to reality. Step 4 of the Six-Step Leadership Challenge is where you stop reacting to today and start designing the systems, habits, and calculated leaps that make tomorrow inevitable. This isn't about crafting a flawless plan, and it's not about waiting for full control, full approval, or perfect clarity. Progress doesn't reward the most polished strategy deck. It rewards the leaders who move first and learn faster. That's why you're not building a corporate strategy deck here, you're building something far more powerful: a living, breathing set of low-risk leadership trials that move you forward, now.

This is your launch point into action. Small bold tests. Fast feedback. Smart adjustments. Real progress.

You're not waiting anymore. You're leading.

The Mindset Shift That Changes Everything

Tanya had already done the work. She'd clarified her vision, reclaimed her calendar, and started shedding some of the "fixer" reflexes that made her the go-to person for every fire drill.

But one pattern still lingered.

In her weekly senior leadership sync, she always deferred. Tanya knew the numbers better than anyone, and she had the clearest pulse on operations, but when strategic questions hit the table, she'd hold back, letting others steer while she filled in the gaps.

It wasn't a knowledge gap. It was a permission gap.

In one of our sessions, she said it outright: "I know I'm leading. But I don't always feel like it."

That's when we designed a five-minute trial. Not a performance. Not a speech. Just one intentional experiment to shift how she showed up in the room.

I asked her: "If you didn't defer this time, if you stepped into the lead, what would that actually look like?"

She hesitated, then started listing background facts and summaries.

I stopped her. "Not the background. The lead."

She nodded, thinking it through. "Okay... I'd do what the CEO usually does. I'd set the frame for the decision, lay out the tradeoffs clearly, and point to a recommendation."

"Exactly," I said. "Now say it like you're already doing it. Say it like the room is waiting on you."

She smiled, took a breath, and stepped into it.

That's exactly what she did the next morning. She picked one high-stakes topic operational tradeoffs for a new customer segment and went first. She framed the decision, named the tradeoffs, and offered a clear recommendation. Then she stopped talking. There was no hedging, no overexplaining, and no circling back. She didn't just offer input. She modeled leadership, and the room shifted. People started responding to her differently. But more importantly, she started seeing herself differently. That five-minute experiment broke the old story that she was there to support, not steer.

The next week, she returned to our session with a different tone. More grounded and more certain, not because the organization had changed, but because she had. The way she carried herself. The way she spoke. The way she moved through decisions. That one visible moment had become a new internal truth: She didn't need to be handed authority. She just needed to take it.

Coach's Commentary

You don't need a full transformation to lead differently. You need one bold moment to break the old pattern, and one clear action to start writing the new one.

That's what Tanya found. A moment of visible authority led to a shift in presence, which revealed a new internal truth that didn't need a new title to be real. Not external validation, but **internal evidence** that she could act, lead, and drive forward without waiting.

That's the power of leaning in. One bold moment. One small shift. A professional identity recalibrated. And here's what I tell people who say, "30 days isn't enough for an experiment."

30 days is plenty, if you set it up right.

Because sometimes you don't even need 30 days. Sometimes you just need five minutes.

Tanya didn't need a month-long rollout to change how she was seen. She needed one clear moment of ownership. One decision to speak first, frame the tradeoffs, and lead the room. Her goal wasn't to transform everything overnight; it was to be seen differently, and it started with one five-minute experiment. That's the work. That's the shift. That's the job, well done.

Reframing the L.E.A.D. Lab: Welcome to My Laboratory

You're not just building a plan. You're designing a Leadership Lab, a place where your boldest ideas get tested, not just talked about. That's why Step 4 of the Six-Step Leadership Challenge isn't about downloading another strategy template. It's about experimenting on purpose. It's about building the conditions, cadence, and clarity to move faster than the chaos around you.

And the lab you're building? It runs on four distinct but connected workstreams, which we call the L.E.A.D. Lab.

L: Lean Into Your Story

Prototype experiments that reconnect you to your core identity, clarify your boldest vision, and translate it into strategic focus with real-world traction. You can't shape the future if you're still guessing who you are.

E: Empower Your Story

Run systems-level experiments that scale your leadership through others using delegation sprints, ownership loops, and delivery architecture that drives results. Real power isn't about control, it's about design that delivers.

A: Amplify Your Story

Design experiments that shape your team's experience of leadership through culture signals, emotional intelligence, and interface systems that connect people to purpose. This is where leadership becomes contagious, not just effective.

D: Durability for Your Story

Build sustainable momentum through executive presence, personal brand, and the energy systems that protect your capacity while extending your impact. Your influence won't last if your life can't hold it.

These four workstreams aren't phases. They're more like swimlanes in your lab, all running simultaneously. And what runs through them? Experiments. But experiments without structure become noise. So here's how we bring strategy into the lab.

Why Strategy Feels Like a Buzzword Salad (and How to Fix It)

You've heard it before: "We need a strategic plan."

But what you get is a glorified to-do list dressed up in timelines, bullet points, and jargon. People throw around terms like *planning, strategy, tactics, goals,* and *vision,* **like they're interchangeable. They're not.**

Strategy isn't planning. Planning is what to do. Strategy is why, where, and how to apply pressure for maximum impact.

Inside the L.E.A.D. Lab, we stop the swirl because when you confuse strategy with planning, you don't just waste time, you lose traction. When leaders confuse these terms, they end up leading at the task level instead of the leverage level. So, here's how we break it down:

Vision
What future are you building?

↓

Goals (Milestones)
What does success look like in 90 days?

↓

Objectives
What outcomes move the system forward?

↓

Experiments
What small, strategic test will you run?

↓

Tasks
What actions will bring the experiment to life?

From Vision to Velocity: The Strategy Stack

This is how we structure your 90-Day Leadership Lab:

- **Vision.** What future are you building? A vivid, energizing picture of what leadership looks like when you're fully aligned.

- **Goals (Milestones).** What does success look like in 90 days? Your key targets across the four L.E.A.D. lanes, what you'll aim to achieve, and how you'll know you're progressing.

- **Objectives.** What outcomes will move the system toward those goals in the next 30, 60, or 90 days? These are your leverage points. Designed to shift momentum, not just check a box.

- **Experiments.** What small, strategic test will help you learn or make progress right now? Each one is framed with a question, a hypothesis, a time limit, a measure, and a way to reflect and adapt.

- **Tasks.** What work will you do inside the experiment each week? These are the focused actions that bring the test to life, not a to-do list, but intentional motion toward insight.

This stack isn't corporate theory. It's how real leadership accelerates in real time. Because when you clarify each layer, when you separate vision from goals, and goals from experiments, you don't just build alignment. You build momentum.

The L.E.A.D. Lab Map

Imagine a simple grid: four rows, five columns. The rows represent the four domains of your Leadership Lab, **Lean, Empower, Amplify, and Durability**, the core arenas where your experiments live and leadership grows. The columns span your next cycle of action: **30 days, 60 days, 90 days, 90-day goals**, and finally, **What Did We Learn?**

This map becomes your visual operating system. In each 30/60/90 cell, you'll define a focused objective, choose one or two smart experiments, name how you'll measure progress, and run a quick mini-retrospective to assess what shifted and what needs to scale, tweak, or die. The **90-Day Goals** column lets you stay aligned on your milestone outcomes, while the **What Did We Learn?** column is your pause-and-harvest moment, a built-in checkpoint to make meaning from momentum.

You don't need a perfect map. You need a working map, one that's alive with movement, iteration, and insight, because this isn't a project plan; this is a leadership lab. A prototype engine. A map that gets smarter every time you run it.

THE L.E.A.D. LAB MAP

DOMAINS	30 DAYS	60 DAYS	90-DAYS	90-DAY GOALS	WHAT DID WE LEARN?
LEAN					
EMPOWER					
AMPLIFY					
DURABILITY					

Coach's Commentary

Big strategy decks impress people in boardrooms, but living strategies? They evolve, adapt, and accelerate real-world momentum. That's what we're building here.

Why Small Experiments Beat Big Plans

Ambitious leaders often default to big plans. They feel strategic, responsible, and safe because they delay the risk of action. But impactful leadership isn't measured by how impressive your planning deck looks. It's measured by how quickly you learn, adapt, and create traction.

Big plans usually collapse under their own weight the moment reality changes. Small, strategic experiments are different because they create learning before commitment. They create traction before bureaucracy. They create movement before resistance has time to set in.

A 30-day leadership experiment, on the other hand, doesn't need executive sign-off, a 12-slide business case, or an annual review cycle. It needs one clear question, one bold hypothesis, and one deliberate action. This is why you're not building a strategy deck right now. You're building a strategy test lab.

Every 30-day experiment gives you clarity:

- Data, not opinions.

- Momentum, not meetings.

- Insight, not perfection.

And in a world where uncertainty is the only certainty, small, fast learning beats big, slow planning every time. You don't have to guess the perfect path. You just have to move and learn while you move. Because the leaders who survive long term aren't the ones who guess best. They're the ones who learn fastest.

Coach's Commentary

Big plans look good in theory. Small experiments create results in reality. Lead where it counts.

What Makes It a Real Experiment?

I have seen plenty of leaders say, *"Let's try it and see what happens."* Or *"Let's run a pilot and see if it works."* But most of the time, there's no real question. No clear hypothesis. No defined way to measure success or failure. And six months later, when I ask what they learned... They can't remember what they were testing, what changed, or if anything stuck at all.

That's not an experiment. That's drift.

If we want to build strategic leadership habits, and not just hopeful activity, we need a better blueprint. Just like your fifth-grade science fair poster, a real experiment has structure, discipline, and purpose.

The ⑥-STEP Leadership Experiment Canvas

Question or Problem:	The experiment in action: Capture the results of the experiment
Hypothesis: We believe that if we: _____ Then we will get _____ Within _____ Because it means: _____	**Analyze the Results:** ☐ Yes, it works! ☐ No, it does not work ☐ Sort of works, Needs tweaking ☐ Inconclusive
The Experiment Design: What: How: Team: Duration: Metrics:	**Next Steps:** What is your next move

Here are the six parts that turn "trying something" into actual leadership insight:

1. **The Question.** What are you testing or trying to learn? Example: "Will empowering my team leads to own their priorities improve delivery speed?"

2. **The Hypothesis.** What do you believe will happen, and why? Example: "If I step back and ask strategic questions instead of solving problems, they'll take more ownership, because I'm shifting the expectation."

3. **The Test Move.** What's the smallest, boldest, fastest action that would prove or disprove it? This isn't a department-wide rollout. It's one sharp, intentional move designed to get signal fast.

4. **The Measure.** How will you track progress or outcomes? Think behavior, not just numbers. What will *look* or *feel* different if it's working?

5. **The Timeframe.** When will this start and stop? Keep it to 30 days or less. Long enough for meaningful feedback. Short enough to stay focused.

6. **The Reflection.** What did you learn, and what's your next move? This is the part that too many leaders skip. It's also where insight and momentum live.

THE L.E.A.D. LAB MAP

DOMAINS	30 DAYS	60 DAYS	90-DAYS	90-DAY GOALS	WHAT DID WE LEARN?
LEAN					
EMPOWER					
AMPLIFY					
DURABILITY					

Experiment: Break Bottlenecks in Decision Flow

Objective: Increase decision velocity and reduce dependency on my input

Question/Problem: Are decisions stalling because people wait on me to weigh in?

Hypothesis: If I give one direct report full decision authority with coaching, not micromanagement, they'll move faster and build confidence.

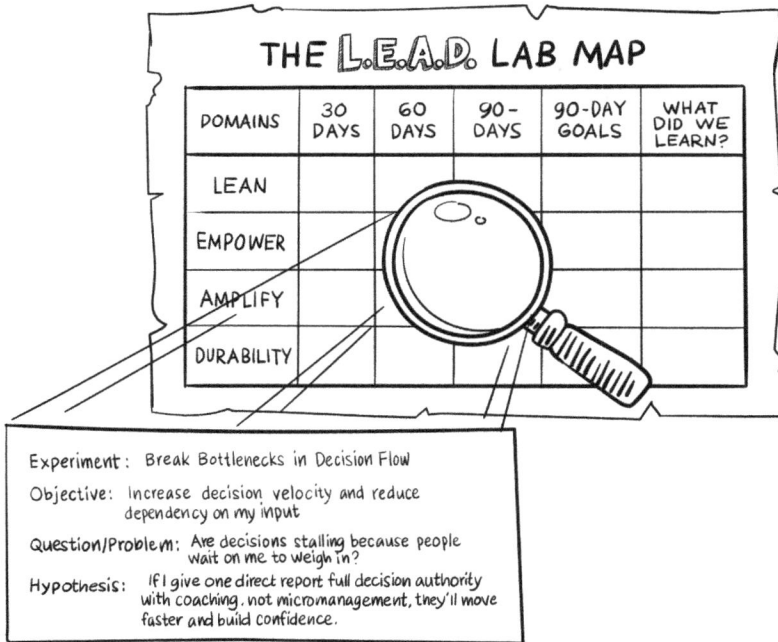

Once you've got these six, you're not just reacting. You're learning, adapting, and leading with intent. And when you run these experiments every 30 days? That's when the flywheel kicks in.

Introducing the 30-Day Flywheel

Leadership plans often fail because they try to predict too much, too soon. You cannot architect a full transformation with perfect foresight or guess every obstacle, every twist, every opportunity. But you can build a system that learns as it moves.

That's the power of the 30-Day Flywheel.

Each 30-day cycle in your L.E.A.D. Lab is a self-contained flywheel, one full turn through action, reflection, and adjustment. Not a hamster wheel. A learning loop.

THE L.E.A.D. LAB MAP

DOMAINS	30 DAYS	60 DAYS	90 - DAYS	90-DAY GOALS	WHAT DID WE LEARN?
LEAN					
EMPOWER					
AMPLIFY					
DURABILITY					

30-DAY Flywheel 1 **30-DAY Flywheel 2** **30-DAY Flywheel 3**

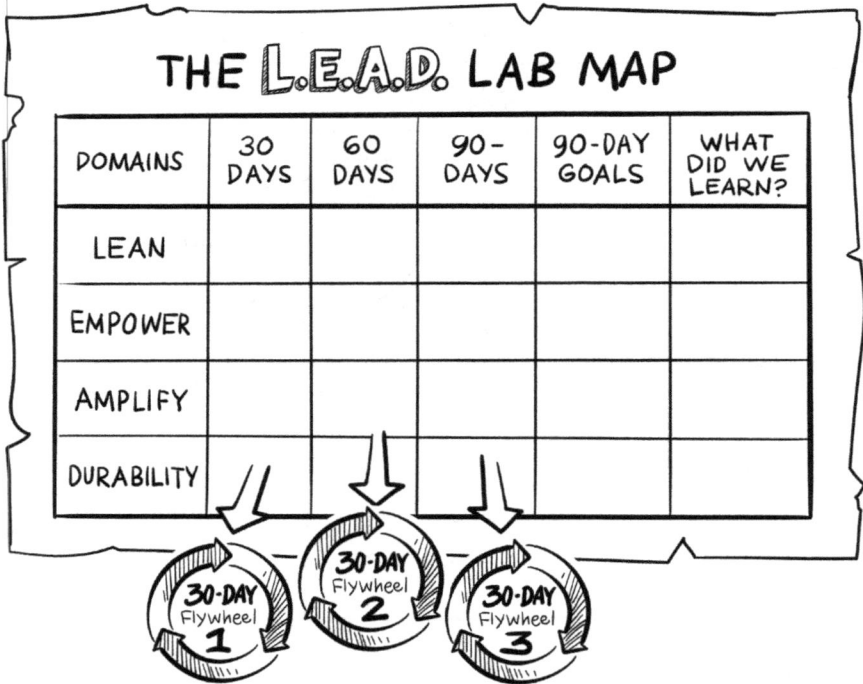

The flywheel starts with **Try Something**, a bold, simple experiment, then moves to **Track What Happens**, where you capture the reality, not the theory. From there, it flows to **Reflect and Adjust**—what worked, what didn't and then spins into your **Next Move**, where you're better informed, sharper, and faster than before.

The faster you turn it, the stronger your leadership gets. The 30-Day Flywheel is simple:

- Every 30 days, you run small experiments.

- Every 30 days, you reflect on what worked, what didn't, and what surprised you.

- Every 30 days, you adjust your next moves based on real learning, not guesses.

It's not about spinning in place. It's about tightening the loop between action, reflection, and evolution. The 30-Day Flywheel is not a nice-to-have in leadership anymore; it's a necessity. It gives you three powerful advantages:

- **Speed:** You stop waiting for perfect clarity and start learning faster than the environment changes.

- **Focus:** You prioritize small, strategic moves that matter, not endless meetings about possible futures.

- **Resilience:** You treat obstacles as data points, not dead ends.

Leadership experiments live inside this flywheel. You try, you learn, and you adjust. Not once a year. Every month.

And the leaders who build that rhythm, the ones who create momentum flywheels that spin faster and stronger every 30 days, are the ones who stop reacting to change and start shaping it.

Coach's Commentary

You don't need a crystal ball. You need a flywheel that learns faster than the world changes. I've watched clients build this rhythm mid-chaos and mid-doubt. They didn't wait to feel ready. They just ran a 30-day test and let the motion do the work.

Bonus Toolkit: Design Better Experiments With AI

You've got the framework, but if you want to supercharge it, we built a companion tool to help you design smarter, faster experiments that actually move the needle.

The Design Better Experiments With AI is packed with:

- Strategic prompts that sharpen your thinking

- Templates to turn bold ideas into testable moves

- Success patterns pulled from real-world leaders who made it work

It's not required, but if you're ready to stop theorizing and start testing like a pro, it's here for you. Find the download link at the end of the book or on our resource site. No filler. Just a powerful toolkit to accelerate your next step.

Lean Into Your Story: Build the Leadership Vision You're Meant to Live

The Lean lane is your identity lane, but don't mistake that for introspection alone.

By now, you've already named your leadership story and vision. You've mapped what you want to stand for, what outcomes matter, and how you want to show up. But defining it isn't enough. Now it's time to test it.

This is where strategy gets personal. It's where you stop reacting to the version of leadership others expect and start aligning to the leader you're here to become. That means vision, yes, but also strategy, goals, focus, visibility, and traction.

Lean isn't just about knowing your story. It's about shaping the next chapter intentionally and testing whether it holds up in the real world. Every experiment in this lane is designed to shift your story, your direction, or your clarity. But don't start with an activity. Start with an objective. Ask yourself: *What needs to become true about my leadership identity, my direction, or my focus in the next 30 days?* That's your objective. Then you run a short, strategic experiment to move you toward it.

The Lean lane is the strategy spine of your lab. Vision is where it starts, but clarity, traction, and visibility are how it earns real estate in your leadership operating system.

10 Sample Objectives for *Lean Into Your Story*

These sample objectives are here to jumpstart your next 30/60/90 days. Each one is an experiment, something you *test*, *learn from*, and *adapt*. And they come in three flavors:

- **Individual:** focused on how you clarify vision, lead, and create traction

- **Team:** designed to shift how your team aligns, executes, and responds

- **Both:** moves that sharpen your leadership *and* ripple visibly across others

Don't try to run them all. Pick the ones that will move the needle now, or design your own to match your role, your team, and your terrain.

1. **Clarify a vivid 12–18 month leadership vision** *(individual)*. Define what your leadership will *look, feel, and deliver* over the next year. Anchor it in real outcomes, not just aspirations.

2. **Translate your vision into four 90-day strategic milestones** *(individual)*. Break your long-term direction into quarterly goals tied to outcomes you can influence directly.

3. **Identify one key misalignment between your current role and your ideal leadership story** *(individual)*. Spot the gap between how you're currently spending your time and where you want your impact to live.

4. **Build traction around one top strategic priority** *(Both)*. Choose one bold idea and move it out of your notes and into real-world execution.

5. **Create visibility for your leadership direction with key stakeholders** *(Team)*. Socialize your vision or goals across your team, peers, or boss, and get feedback to sharpen alignment.

6. **Diagnose what's holding your strategy back from momentum** *(Team)*. Uncover where your vision is fuzzy, your goals are vague, or your priorities aren't moving.

7. **Test whether your vision resonates across your team** *(Team)*. Share your leadership direction and track how well it energizes, aligns, and mobilizes others.

8. **Build a "strategy spine" that connects your vision to your weekly actions** *(individual)*. Create a system that helps you track whether your daily focus actually supports your leadership trajectory.

9. **Reclaim 90 minutes per week for "vision work"** *(individual)*. Carve out protected time to sharpen your strategic direction and stress-test your roadmap.

10. **Refine your personal leadership brand to align with your future story** *(individual)*. Get clear on how others perceive you now, and whether that aligns with the story you're writing next.

Four Sample Experiments in the Lean Lane

🔬 Experiment 1: Translate Vision Into a Strategy Stack

- **Type:** Individual

- **Question/Problem:** Is my 12–18 month leadership vision clear and actionable enough to guide strategy today?

- **Hypothesis:** If I break my vision into 90-day goals and socialize one of them, it will clarify focus and invite productive alignment.

- **Action Plan:** Draft a 30-60-90 roadmap for one domain (e.g., stakeholder trust). Share it with one key stakeholder or peer and ask for input.

- **Timeframe:** 30 days

- **Measure:** Quality of feedback received, clarity of follow-up actions, and alignment in next meeting or check-in.

- **Reflection:** What landed clearly? What caused confusion? Did this test sharpen the next steps or signal a need to refine direction?

🔬 Experiment 2: Define Your 90-Day Strategic Priorities

- **Type:** Individual

- **Question/Problem:** Am I investing time and energy in what's most strategic for the next 90 days?

- **Hypothesis:** If I identify and realign around three clear outcomes, my time and decision-making will become more focused and effective.

- **Action Plan:** Run a "priority inversion" audit and log 7 days of time spent vs. top 90-day goals. Reallocate 20% of time to one top priority.

- **Timeframe:** 30 days

- **Measure:** Hours reallocated, momentum gained, or visible traction toward the 90-day goal.

- **Reflection:** Did the shift generate progress, clarity, or visible traction? What's worth scaling or adjusting in the next flywheel?

🔬 Experiment 3: Create Strategic Visibility for the Work That Matters

- **Type:** Both

- **Question/Problem:** Do my stakeholders understand what matters most in my leadership focus?

- **Hypothesis:** If I share one strategic message in different formats, I'll learn which channels and framings build better buy-in.

- **Action Plan:** Choose one message aligned with a 90-day goal. Test it in three formats: live meeting, written update, and decision framing.

- **Timeframe:** 30 days

- **Measure:** Stakeholder response, message clarity, and whether the message got repeated or reinforced by others.

- **Reflection:** Which channel landed best? What shifted in energy, ownership, or alignment? What should be my go-to visibility move?

🔬 Experiment 4: Design a Strategic Feedback Loop

- **Type:** Individual

- **Question/Problem:** Am I pressure-testing my assumptions before scaling a strategic direction?

- **Hypothesis:** If I surface and test one assumption with trusted feedback, I'll strengthen my direction and reduce risk.

- **Action Plan:** Build a five-slide preview deck outlining my strategy or shift. Walk it through with two trusted peers.

- **Timeframe:** 30 days

- **Measure:** Strength and specificity of feedback, number of assumptions validated or refined.

- **Reflection:** What did this conversation confirm, challenge, or reframe? Where do I pivot or double down based on what I heard?

We're not just building confidence here; we're building strategic traction by making vision executable.

If you want to go deeper, I've built a full Leadership Experiment Library: A curated set of tools designed to help you test your clarity, direction, and leadership story across all four L.E.A.D. swimlanes. You'll find a full list of experiments and how to access the library in the **Resources** section at the back of the book. It's designed to help you take what you're reading and turn it into motion, right where it counts.

But you don't need a full playbook to begin. You just need one meaningful objective and the guts to run the first test. The experiment you run next doesn't have to solve everything. It just has to solve for motion because clarity isn't something you wait for; it's something you build by moving.

Driving Question

> What bold test case could you run in the next 30 days, just for you?

Your Coaching Question From Jim

> What's one leadership move you've been putting off because it's small, because it's personal, or because it might actually work?

Mini Challenge: The 30-Day Experiment Flywheel

> Download Worksheet: W7 – 30-Day Experiment Flywheel

You've just learned how the 90-Day Ascent Grid works, now it's time to get your hands dirty. Design yours using the Six-Step Leadership Experiment Canvas.

- **Question or Problem:** What are you testing?

- **Hypothesis:** What do you believe will happen, and why?

- **Action Plan:** What exactly will you do, and when?

- **Time Frame:** 30 days. No more.

- **Measures:** How will you track progress, surprises, and pivots?

- **Reflection:** How will you decide what's next?

Then run it. Not quietly. Not hypothetically. In deliberate, visible motion. At the end of the 30 days, ask yourself:

- What happened?

- What changed?

- What did you learn?

- What would you double down on, or ditch?

The leaders who shift the fastest aren't the ones with the best plan at the start. They're the ones who launched the first **pilo**t while everyone else was still debating. This isn't homework. This is your first mile marker toward a different leadership story. Start the rhythm now, and you'll build momentum faster than you can believe.

Final Reframe: Vision Without Action Is Just a Pretty Lie

You've named your vision and you've sketched your future, but until you run your first action test, it's still just theory. There's no such thing as transformation without motion, there's no leadership growth without action, and there's no momentum until you stop thinking and start testing.

You don't need a perfect strategy. You need a real one. You need to get in the arena, run a 30-day move, and learn from what happens next. Because leaders don't rise on potential. They rise on pattern. And patterns start with one bold move, repeated, refined, and scaled.

If you remember nothing else from this chapter, remember this:

You don't win by waiting for clarity. You win by running the first experiment while everyone else is still waiting.

This is the part I love most in coaching: When someone stops circling the idea and finally steps in. That first test might be messy, but it's theirs, and that's when it gets real. Your growth journey just shifted from ideas to action.

Now it's time to build the systems and support around you that make those **shifts** durable, visible, and scalable. That's where we're headed next. In Chapter 8, we'll move into the next swimlane: **Empower Your Story**, where you stop trying to do everything yourself and start designing systems that multiply your reach through others.

CHAPTER 8

Build a Team That Thinks Without You

If your team needs you in every decision,
you didn't build a team; you built dependence.

– Jim Saliba

Control doesn't just collapse out of nowhere. It collapses when it grips too tightly. It suffocates itself.

Hold too many decisions, too many solutions, too many answers, and you won't just bottleneck the work, you'll choke your own growth. You become the ceiling your team can't rise above.

If you're still the smartest person in the room, you're not elevating, you're limiting. And if projects always bottleneck at your desk, you're not empowering anyone. You're just replicating a bigger, slower version of yourself.

This is where *Empower Your Story* begins inside the L.E.A.D. Lab: Shift from doing it yourself to scaling others. Stop hoarding excellence, and start designing it into your systems. Build the machine. Don't be the machine. Because clarity, trust, and rhythm aren't accidents, they're architecture, and empowerment isn't about stepping back and hoping for the best. It's about stepping up into structure, ownership, and velocity that can survive without you at the center.

You're not here to be indispensable. You're here to develop the kind of team that accelerates even faster when you step aside.

Michael's Story

You've met Michael before. Senior Director of Operations. Trusted. Respected. Essential. Maybe too essential.

No matter how many systems he built or how many priorities he tried to delegate, projects and blockers kept finding their way back to him. One night, well past hours, he messaged me: "I know I need to get out of the weeds, but every time I try, the whole thing grinds to a halt. It's like I'm the engine and the brakes at the same time."

He wasn't wrong. Michael wasn't leading a team, he was running a hub. Everything flowed through him. Every decision paused at his desk, and every fire drill somehow landed in his inbox. He wasn't expanding capacity. He *was* the capacity. And it was burning him out. So, we broke the pattern. We took one moment, one test, one chance to start telling a different story.

Michael had a direct report, Sasha, who was smart, steady, and ready for more. She'd been supporting a high-visibility, cross-functional initiative for months, but Michael still made every final call, approved all the updates, handled every escalation, and even steered committee decks.

So we flipped it.

For 30 days, Sasha would lead the initiative end-to-end, and Michael would step back completely. Together, they defined success criteria, built a simple scoreboard, and agreed on a weekly coaching-style check-in, focused purely on unblocking challenges, not overriding decisions.

The first week was rough. He sat on his hands during two tense stakeholder conversations where he normally would've stepped in. But he didn't. In week two, Sasha made a judgment call he wouldn't have made, and it worked. She solved a blocker, took a risk, and earned more airspace. By week four, she was running meetings he used to lead. She wasn't just managing the work. She was owning it.

Then came the turning point.

"The update deck hit the CEO's desk," Michael told me, "and my name wasn't on it. It didn't need to be. That's when it clicked."

That single experiment didn't just clear his calendar; it rewired his culture. Decisions moved without him, ownership rose, and the team stopped waiting for instructions and started building momentum of their own.

Michael didn't just get time back. He got trust forward.

That's empowerment. Not stepping back, but stepping up to build the system that moves without you at the center.

What It Means to Empower Your Story

Inside the L.E.A.D. Laboratory, **Empower** is your systems track. It's where you stop being the engine and start becoming the architect. It's where leadership stops being a personal performance and starts becoming a platform.

Empowerment doesn't mean letting go. It means designing systems that create trust on purpose. It's about

- Building shared clarity, so people know what they own, and how their work fits the whole.

- Creating repeatable rhythms, so your team stops playing calendar Tetris and starts moving like a crew with a shared GPS.

- Designing trust into your workflows, so people act with confidence even when you're not in the room.

Let me bring that into focus. When you empower through the lab you do the following:

- You clarify ownership. Because fuzzy roles lead to fuzzy execution.

- You install decision structures, so not every question circles back to you.

- You delegate in a way that stretches people's thinking, not just their task list.

This isn't about disappearing. It's about building the wiring that keeps momentum flowing, even when you're not the one flipping the switch. That's how empowerment starts: with decisions moving through others.

Zooming Out: Where Execution Lives

But to truly scale your impact, you need more than delegation. You need execution systems that can deliver without you in the room. This lane isn't just about empowering people. It's about *operationalizing your leadership*. It's where execution lives and where your boldest ideas stop floating in strategy decks and start showing up in calendars, meetings, decisions, and results.

If *Lean into Your Story* is where you define your direction, then *Empower Your Story* is where that direction becomes executable, etched into systems, rhythms, and decision flows that move faster than you can. It's your engine room, where clarity turns into cadence, trust turns into traction, and you stop doing and start building a system that does the doing for you.

Because if your team can't see where you're winning, they'll default to busyness instead of progress.

If You Can't See It, You Can't Lead It

Let's bring this into sharp focus:

Dashboards tell you what's happening. Scoreboards tell you what matters.

You've seen it before, maybe you're living it now. A dashboard with 27 tabs, charts that no one trusts, and metrics that show up late, change weekly, or spark more debate than decision.

Most dashboards are built for review, not for action. They're packed with data, but they don't drive behavior. They inform, but they don't move. And when leaders rely on dashboards alone, momentum dies in the spreadsheet. That's why you've seen the word *scoreboard* show up again and again in this book. It's not by accident, but by design, because a good **scoreboard** answers four questions instantly:

1. **What game are we playing?**

2. **Are we winning?**

3. **How much time do we have left?**

4. **What do we need to do next?**

That's it. If your team can't answer those four questions without a PowerPoint, you don't have a scoreboard; you have a reference file.

Dashboards are for analysts, scoreboards are for players, and if you want execution, you need players to move, not just understand.

This shift comes straight from The 4 Disciplines of Execution (4DX), and I've seen it play out in workshop after workshop. Just last week, a team told me they were tracking performance in a spreadsheet so bloated they couldn't tell what was current, what was accurate, or what actually mattered. That's not leadership visibility, that's spreadsheet noise.

A well-designed **scoreboard**, often a single slide or even a whiteboard, shows *what matters now*, who's accountable, and where the needle is.

- It connects directly to your **lead measures**, not just lagging outcomes.

- It's updated frequently, ideally weekly.

- Most importantly, **your team can read it and act on it** without translation.

If you've been spending hours building a dashboard no one uses, stop. Build a scoreboard instead.

You'll see this again, in depth, in **Chapter 11: Action + Reaction**, where we introduce the Cadence of Accountability and show how real teams use live scoreboards to fuel weekly learning loops. But here, in Chapter 8, is where you start experimenting with visibility and execution, in the now.

> ## Coach's Commentary: If You Can't Name It, You Can't Lead It
>
> If you can't name your top three priorities and their status without a dashboard, you're not leading, you're reacting. Authority isn't about knowing everything. It's about knowing what matters, on demand.

Sarah's Scoreboard Shift

Sarah didn't need help getting things done. She was the definition of reliable. Her calendar was color-coded, her updates airtight, and her team… well, they were waiting.

Waiting for her review. Waiting for her green light. Waiting for her to run the whole show. And that was the problem.

In one of our sessions, she let it slip. "I feel like I'm the system. If I stop moving, everything stalls."

She wasn't exaggerating. Her so-called "dashboard" was a multi-tab spreadsheet graveyard, half-updated, rarely trusted, and visible only to her.

So, I asked, "If you weren't the system, what would be?"

She paused, thinking. "I guess… we'd need something visible. Something real. Something they could track without me."

"Exactly," I said. "You don't need a dashboard. You need a scoreboard."

She raised an eyebrow.

"A scoreboard tells you the game you're playing, whether you're winning, how much time is left, and what to do next. Dashboards show data. Scoreboards drive behavior."

So, we designed a small experiment. Just one initiative. I asked her to pull the team together and pose one question: *What are the two or three lead indicators that tell us this is working?* They built it together. They debated what red, yellow, and green meant. They set a simple cadence: weekly check-ins, 15 minutes max, and score-only updates. No status novels and no Sarah-saving-the-day.

The first meeting was rough. Sarah still jumped in to clarify. To fix. To steer. But by week two, she let the silence stretch, and her team stepped in. By week four, they were adjusting their own targets, owning the metrics, and moving forward without her as the bottleneck.

In the next session, she smiled and said, "I finally felt like I could breathe. And they looked... proud."

That was her shift from leader-as-hero to leader-as-architect.

Coach's Commentary

You don't scale leadership by being the system. You scale by building one others can run.

Sarah didn't just build a scoreboard. She built a structure her team could own through one small test that rewired trust, accountability, and rhythm. The results? Real progress, less rescuing, and more room to lead.

Why Empowerment Experiments Matter

You don't build an empowered team with trust falls and slogans. You build it by rewiring the system underneath the behaviors you're frustrated by, the ones that stall projects, bottleneck decisions, and bury progress in status updates.

Here's the pattern I see over and over in, so called, high-performance teams:

- **No clear ownership?** Projects stall, accountability gets murky, and everyone waits for someone else to decide.

- **Dependence on the leader?** Progress bottlenecks. People stay busy, but no one moves without you in the room.

- **Meetings with no traction?** Updates feel productive, but they're just noise. Everyone's talking, no one's deciding, and nothing's moving. It's all comment, no action, like a group Slack thread with snacks. The only outcome? Another invite. Can't this just be an email?

- **Dashboards with a thousand metrics, but no scoreboard?** No one knows if they're winning. They drown in data and stop playing to win.

These aren't people problems, they're design problems, and if you don't redesign the structure, no amount of motivational speeches or "delegating more" will fix it.

That's why in the L.E.A.D. Lab, we don't "talk about trust." We **design** trust. We **build** ownership. We intentionally **install** rhythm and visibility. And we do it one experiment at a time. Small, testable changes that create repeatable wins, until the system runs on momentum, not micromanagement. Because empowered cultures aren't willed into being. They're engineered, prototype by prototype.

Visual Diagnostic: The Bottleneck Stack

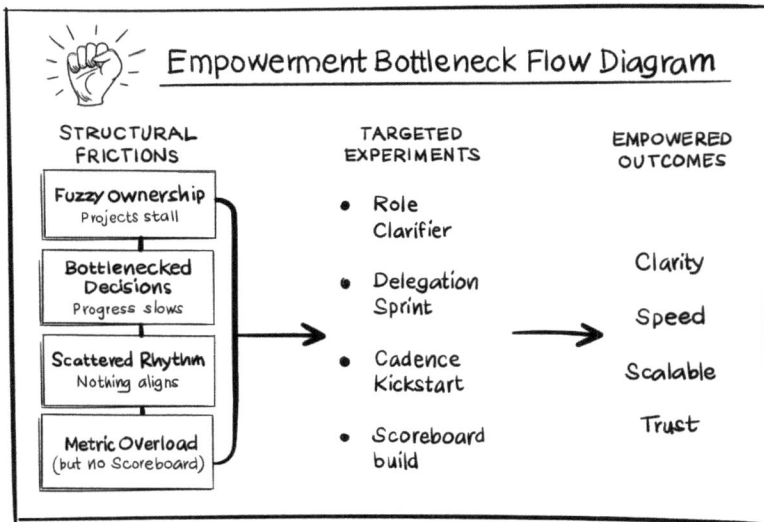

Empowerment Bottleneck Flow Diagram

STRUCTURAL FRICTIONS	TARGETED EXPERIMENTS	EMPOWERED OUTCOMES
Fuzzy Ownership (Projects stall)	• Role Clarifier	
Bottlenecked Decisions (Progress slows)	• Delegation Sprint	Clarity
Scattered Rhythm (Nothing aligns)	• Cadence Kickstart	Speed / Scalable
Metric Overload (but no Scoreboard)	• Scoreboard build	Trust

Imagine a vertical stack of four blocks, each one a pressure point that quietly sabotages your speed and autonomy:

- Fuzzy Ownership → Projects stall

- Bottlenecked Decisions → Progress slows

- Scattered Rhythm → Nothing aligns

- Metric Overload (No Scoreboard) → Confusion, no traction

Each layer compounds the one below it.
Now, imagine next to each block is a lever. That lever is an experiment.

- **Role Clarifier Canvas** to fix ownership.

- **Delegation Sprint** to break the bottlenecks.

- **Cadence Kickstart** to restore rhythm.

- **Scoreboard Build** to make progress visible again.

This isn't about working harder; it's about designing smarter, because empowerment isn't a mindset. It's a system. And if your system is stuck in this bottleneck stack, you don't need better people, you need better prototypes.

The Myth We're Breaking

"If I don't do it, it won't get done right."

That's not excellence. That's ego disguised as helpfulness. It may feel noble and necessary, but it's a chokehold on growth. You're not protecting quality. You're blocking it from scaling.

> ## *Coach's Commentary: Progress Isn't Faster Alone; It's Stronger Together*
>
> Grip tighter, and yes, you'll move faster. For all of five minutes. But leadership isn't about five minutes. It's about five quarters. Five years. Five hundred decisions that get made well without you. Your ceiling isn't your speed. It's how fast others move when you're not in the room.

The Pain Behind It

It's not just about control. It's about scars. Scars from the project that blew up when you delegated. Scars from the team member who dropped the ball, and the fallout you absorbed. Scars from a culture where mistakes aren't coached, they're punished.

So, you started playing it safe. You told yourself it was faster to just do it. You framed it as "being thorough." You convinced yourself this season would pass, and *then* you'd start letting go.

But the plan didn't stick, and now you're buried chasing loose ends, cleaning up silent failures, and redoing work you never should've touched again. Not because you're not capable, but because the system never changed. You're stuck holding it all together, while everything around you keeps slipping through the cracks, and the longer you stay in the loop of over-functioning, the lower your ceiling becomes.

The only way out? A smarter test. A deliberate shift. One experiment that starts loosening the grip and rewiring the way work flows through others, not just through you.

Empower Your Story: Build Systems That Scale Without You

You're not the system, but if everything runs through you, every decision, every escalation, every fire drill, then you've accidentally become one, and systems that rely on a single point of contact eventually break. This lane is where we fix that.

Empower Your Story isn't about spreadsheets, org charts, or delegation theater. It's about execution architecture. The kind that moves decisions forward, turns meetings into action, and builds momentum without needing your fingerprints on every deliverable.

Your job isn't to be available but to be scalable, and scalability starts with structure. Not more effort, not more hours, and definitely not another inbox rule. This is the swimlane where you design the rhythms, handoffs, scoreboards, and systems that drive clarity and progress even when you're off the grid.

But don't jump straight to tools.

This is a common mistake, especially if you come from the software world. I've been there myself. We want to believe the tool is the process and that by installing the software, writing the SOP, or rolling out the template, we're solving the real problem. But tools can't replace clarity. They can only support it. If you don't know what you want to achieve, no tool will get you there, and if you haven't defined what success actually looks like, the best system in the world will just help you execute confusion more efficiently. Start with the real question:

What needs to become true about how your team executes, decides, or delivers in the next 30 days?

That's your objective. Once you've answered that question, you can design the structures and choose the tools that serve it, without letting them dictate your leadership.

10 Sample Objectives in the Empower Lane

Just like in the last chapter, we're offering 10 sample objectives. They're your next smart moves to test, learn, and lead with intention. You'll see the same three types: **Individual**, **Team**, and **Both**, because leadership starts with you but doesn't end there.

Pick what moves. Build what fits.

1. **Clarify roles and decision ownership** *(Team)*. Reduce confusion, map who drives what, and make ownership obvious (and undeniable).

2. **Break bottlenecks in decision flow** *(Both)*. Stop being the approval gate for every choice. Design smart autonomy that is backed by trust.

3. **Create execution rhythms that don't rely on you** *(Team)*. Replace status ping-pong with real cadence. Your absence shouldn't equal paralysis.

4. **Make progress visible with a real scoreboard** *(Team)*. Build tools your team actually looks at, understands, and uses to guide action.

5. **Strengthen the ownership mindset across the team** *(Both)*. Get people solving problems without being asked. Then shine a light on it.

6. **Design handoff systems that don't drop balls** *(Team)*. Stop assuming things will get done. Build rituals that confirm they did.

7. **Reinforce accountability without micromanagement** *(Both)*. Create follow-through systems that track momentum, without breathing down anyone's neck.

8. **Simplify your update process** *(Individual)*. Turn bloated reports into high-signal updates that focus on what's next, not what happened.

9. **Establish lead metrics that drive results** *(Team)*. Help the team focus on what they can influence before the scoreboard locks in the score.

10. Test one cross-functional delivery upgrade *(Team)*. Pilot a shift that improves clarity and speed across teams, then see if it sticks.

Four Sample Experiments for Empower

🔬 Experiment 1: Clarify Roles and Decision Ownership

- **Type:** Team

- **Question/Problem:** Are roles and decision rights clear enough to prevent delays, handoffs, or finger-pointing?

- **Hypothesis:** If we map who drives, decides, and supports key priorities, we'll reduce ambiguity, speed up action, and increase ownership.

- **Action Plan:** Use a Role Clarifier Canvas to define ownership for the team's top three priorities. Pilot the new role map on one live project and observe how it flows.

- **Timeframe:** 30 days

- **Measure:** Number of clarification requests or decision stalls plus team confidence in a short retro or pulse check.

- **Reflection:** Where did clarity increase? Where did confusion still show up? What's worth scaling, tweaking, or ditching?

🔬 Experiment 2: Break Bottlenecks in Decision Flow

- **Type:** Both

- **Question/Problem:** Are decisions stalling because people wait for me to weigh in?

- **Hypothesis:** If I give one direct report full decision authority, with coaching, not micromanagement, they'll move faster and build confidence.

- **Action Plan:** Choose one decision stream that regularly stalls. Run a "Delegation Sprint," define boundaries, assign ownership, and stay in coaching mode while they lead.

- **Timeframe:** 30 days

- **Measure:** Number and speed of decisions made without escalation, plus their self-assessed confidence and clarity after the sprint.

- **Reflection:** Where did the handoff work well? What broke down? What's the next-level shift to build on this?

🔬 Experiment 3: Create Execution Rhythms That Don't Rely on You

- **Type:** Team

- **Question/Problem:** Does execution fall apart when I'm not the one driving it?

- **Hypothesis:** If we shift from status meetings to lead-metric standups, the team will sustain focus and momentum independently.

- **Action Plan:** Replace one weekly status meeting with a lead-metric standup. Assign rotating facilitators and track key drivers of execution.

- **Timeframe:** 30 days

- **Measure:** Meeting consistency, lead metric progress, and whether the rhythm holds without your constant presence.

- **Reflection:** What kept the motion alive? What needs more reinforcement? Is this cadence worth embedding long-term?

🔬 Experiment 4: Make Progress Visible with a Real Scoreboard

- **Type:** Both

- **Question/Problem:** Can the team clearly see what matters most, and whether we're winning?

- **Hypothesis:** If we build a visible scoreboard with lead indicators, we'll create shared clarity and urgency.

- **Action Plan:** Use your Scoreboard Build tool to select 2–3 lead indicators for one initiative. Display the scoreboard weekly and invite the team to rate progress (Red/Yellow/Green).

- **Timeframe:** 30 days

- **Measure:** Team ability to name lead indicators, consistency of updates, and any behavior shifts based on visibility.

- **Reflection:** What worked? What was missed? What would make this scoreboard even more motivating or replicable elsewhere?

We're not just creating better execution. We're proactively building self-healing systems that move faster than you can. If you want more inspiration, I've built a **Leadership Experiment Library** packed with tools that help teams clarify ownership, upgrade execution, and build real autonomy, without waiting for permission. You'll find a full list of Empower experiments in the **Resources section at the back of the book**, along with details on how to access the full library. Or reach out anytime, and we'll talk about how to bring these experiments to life in your org.

Driving Question

☞ What's one thing you're still holding onto that's stalling your people's growth?

Your Coaching Question From Jim

☞ If you disappeared for 30 days, what would break? What might actually get better?

Yes, we know this is a question you've already asked yourself. You first asked this back in Chapter 2, but now you've got the tools to answer it with more honesty, and maybe even come up with a plan.

Mini Challenge: The Delegation Sprint

✎ Download Worksheet: W8 – Delegation Sprint

One task. This week.

- Define what success looks like.

- Share the why, not just the what.

- Check in only to unblock.

Then ask yourself: *What changed? What didn't?*

Reflection Prompts

- What am I still gripping too tightly?

- What story am I telling myself about what will happen if I let go?

- Where could trust be designed instead of assumed?

Your Action Checklist

- Pick one task to delegate

- Define and document success

- Communicate clearly and assign ownership

- Debrief what happened

- Reflect on what held you back

Final Reframe: Let Go to Grow

If you remember nothing else from this chapter, remember this:

You don't scale by doing more. You scale by doing less, better, and building a team that does the rest.

Letting go isn't failure, it's the threshold of real leadership, and delegation isn't dumping work, it's designing growth. You want to lead like a CEO? Then stop clinging like a bottleneck and start building like a builder.

Excellence isn't something you hoard, it's something you engineer into others so it spreads, even when you're not in the room. Trust doesn't begin when people prove they're ready, it begins when you give them the space to rise. Start now. Pick one thing to let go, and when your crew surprises you with how far they run without you? Smile. That's what you built.

Later in Chapter 11, we'll show you how to turn this momentum into a rhythm of learning and iteration because this isn't just about letting go, it's about keeping the loop alive. Next, in Chapter 9, we'll take the next step: shaping the systems, conversations, and culture that amplify your leadership beyond structure, so your story spreads even when you're not in the room.

CHAPTER 9

Shape the Culture, Don't Just Survive It

You're not just running the team,
you're writing its playbook.

– Jim Saliba

You're already shaping your culture, even if you don't mean to.

Every decision you make. Every shortcut you take. Every silence you let slide. It all adds up to a system your people will learn, repeat, and normalize, not because it's ideal, but because it's what you allowed.

You might think you're just solving problems or hitting deadlines, but you're also writing the emotional playbook your team will run with.

The question isn't, **"Are you shaping the culture?"** The question is, **"Are you shaping it on purpose?"**

Coach's Commentary

If you're not choosing your culture, your habits are.

This chapter isn't about slogans or snacks or motivational posters in the hallway. It's about ownership, because culture isn't what you say, it's what you signal, and if you're not signaling with intention, the default wins. And the default? It's usually fear. Fear of incompetence. Fear of looking foolish. Fear of failure. Fear of vulnerability.

This isn't about micromanaging feelings or sending a better all-hands memo. It's about shifting the system your team lives in, emotionally, structurally, and strategically, so your leadership doesn't just echo in meetings, it multiplies when you walk out the door.

I learned this the hard way in my years leading software development teams. Speed was king. Always. And when deadlines loomed (and they always loomed), we defaulted to the same mantra: **Quick and dirty now. Clean it up later.**

Except "later" never came. The shortcuts stuck, testing got skipped, quality faded, and documentation got deferred. But more than that, the culture changed. We didn't just accumulate the mountain of all mountains worth of technical debt. We picked up **cultural debt**. We taught ourselves, and our teams, that rushing was rewarded, and rigor was optional. And that stuck far longer than any code we wrote.

That's what unintentional culture looks like. It's not decided in a workshop. It's built in the day-to-day tradeoffs, workarounds, and habits we never circle back to question. So, if you want to lead differently, not just faster, but better, you have to take the pen back.

It starts here.

The Myth We're Breaking: "Culture is HR's Job"

Let me say this clearly: Culture is not outsourced. And if I can be blunt, in true New Yorker fashion, I do not care how many workshops HR hosts or how many laminated values they slap on the wall; culture is not their job. It starts and ends with you. You want real culture? Own it. Or watch it eat your team alive.

Culture is how your leadership lands when you are not there to explain it. It is what people say when the Zoom call ends. It is how your team responds when things get tense, when you're exhausted, the deadline is tight, and someone just made a mistake. If you think culture is catered lunches and mood boards, you have already lost the plot.

Culture is what happens when people see what you tolerate.

- Who gets protected?

- Who gets blamed?

- Who actually speaks up, and is it safe to?

That is the real scoreboard. What gets rewarded, what gets punished, what gets ignored, what gets promoted, and where conflict actually goes. This is exactly why we did the work in Chapter 3 to read the undercurrent, to see what is unspoken but always there. And why we mapped the terrain in Chapter 4 to understand the structures, incentives, and unwritten rules that shape what actually moves. If you are not shaping those signals, you are surrendering the wheel. You are letting fear, gossip, and leftover trauma from the last regime write the rules of engagement.

Here is what really happens when you leave culture to HR: You create a leadership vacuum, and nature hates a vacuum, so fear fills the gap. Fear of looking foolish. Fear of saying the wrong thing. Fear of taking a risk and getting burned. And once that fear sets in, it is game over. Innovation does not just stall, it hardens. Candor does not just die, it goes underground. People do not just play it safe, they settle. They stop pushing boundaries, stop challenging the status quo, stop growing, and stop moving the work, the team, and themselves forward. They hedge bets, cover their bases, and manage optics instead of driving outcomes.

That shift does not just slow you down; it rots the foundation. Initiative fades. Accountability thins out, the boldest thinkers shut down or leave, and what is left behind is a culture so focused on avoiding mistakes that it forgets how to make real progress. That is why culture is not HR's job; it is yours. It is shaped by what you model, what you allow, what you ignore, and what you reward.

If you want a culture that can handle change, growth, and complexity, you do not get there by telling people to behave better. You get there by making it safe, clear, and expected for them to lead better. Your team does not just need permission. They need to see you go first.

Strategy Doesn't Scale Without Signal

By the time we caught up again, David was deep in it. The pressure was rising, the roadmap was packed, and nothing was moving. This wasn't happening because he didn't have a plan; his strategy was sharp, his metrics lined up, and his leadership team nodded through every slide. And yet initiatives died in silence, meetings ended with yeses that meant no, and every new idea he pitched felt like dragging dead weight uphill.

"I don't get it," he told me. "The plan's solid, but it's like the system itself is resisting."

He wasn't wrong. David wasn't facing a strategy gap. He was stuck in a signal failure. His team wasn't reacting to the logic in his slides; they were reacting to the fear in the system. They were still carrying scars from past leadership, so they were polite in meetings, cautious in execution, and allergic to risk. They weren't saying no out loud, but they weren't saying yes with action either.

I asked him, "What do you think your team is actually reacting to, your plan, or something deeper?"

That stopped him.

He sat back and said, "I think they're reacting to the past. They're polite, but they don't trust it'll stick."

Exactly. David didn't have a strategy problem. He had a signal problem.

So, he stopped adding slides and started reshaping the story, not by turning up the volume, but by tuning the signal. He opened meetings with why the work mattered, not just what the work was. He made space for questions that sounded like resistance but were really fear in disguise. He slowed down to go faster, because trust moves things faster than pressure ever could.

I reminded him of something I tell all my clients: know your audience. Everyone's tuned to the same internal "radio station," **WIIFM: What's In It For Me.** If your message doesn't answer that, it won't land. Once David made that shift, the tone changed. Momentum returned, and people didn't just nod, they actually moved.

David didn't need a sharper message. He needed a stronger mirror.

Coach's Commentary

People don't need perfect leaders. They need permission to move. Because culture doesn't respond to perfection. It responds to permission.

So, let's drop the illusion. **Culture is not a line item. It's the air your team breathes.**

You've already mapped the undercurrent (culture) and the terrain (system). Now comes the amplifier. Because what you reinforce, through people, systems, and signals, either fuels momentum or multiplies confusion. If it's toxic, they'll suffocate, quietly, slowly, and in full compliance. If it's strong? They'll build things you never imagined.

That starts with you.

Culture Is Contagious. So Is Confusion

Remember those four leadership fears from the early chapters? (Incompetence, foolishness, failure, and vulnerability.) If you haven't rewired your leadership environment, those fears don't just stay in your head; they embed into your team. One micromanager creates a fear of incompetence. One avoided conflict feeds fear of failure. One punished risk fuels fear of foolishness. That's why this isn't cosmetic, it's systemic. Amplify is how you build a culture strong enough to absorb uncertainty, and still move.

You already know this in your gut: Culture doesn't live in your values deck. It lives in the day-to-day emotional temperature of your team.

- What do we joke about?

- What do we ignore?

- Who do we listen to, and who gets tuned out?

Every meeting, every decision, every moment of silence... it's all reinforcing something.

If you're not intentional about what's getting amplified, then confusion will take the lead. And confusion spreads fast. When people don't know what the real rules are, they make them up. When they're not sure what success looks like, they play it safe. When your systems are fuzzy, inconsistent, or out of sync, they stop asking questions. They stop offering ideas. They start protecting themselves.

You can feel it in teams that have been burned before. They nod politely and smile through the meeting, but nothing moves afterward because under the surface, they're thinking: "We've seen this before. This won't last. Just survive it."

So the question becomes: what are you actually reinforcing?

Every time you ignore an eye roll at a new idea, you reinforce cynicism. Every time you reward the person who grinds the hardest but collaborates the least, you reinforce heroics over collaboration. Every time you say, "We value trust," but then over-ride your team's decisions… yeah, you just rewrote the cultural playbook, again.

Coach's Commentary

What you allow, you teach. Every time.

This is why we don't just talk about shaping culture. We amplify what matters by tuning three levers that determine whether your strategy sticks or stalls:

1. **People.** Who you hire, how you develop them, and the emotional intelligence you model.

2. **Systems.** The processes that either create clarity and flow or grind your team down.

3. **Culture.** The invisible rules and emotional code your team follows when no one's looking.

That's what this chapter is about. You're not just running the team. **You're writing its code.**

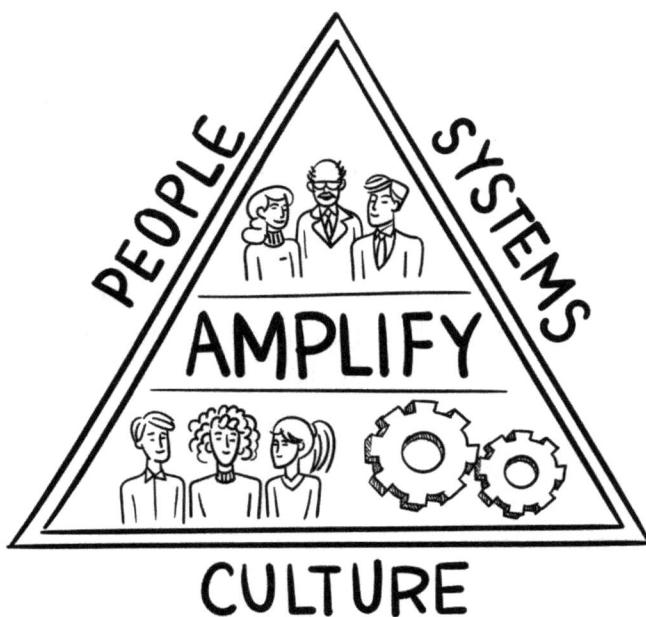

People: You're Not Just Managing Roles, You're Building Belonging

I once coached a VP who kept saying, "Everyone on my team is solid, but we're not accelerating." Turns out, they had hired for *stability* when what they needed was *experimentation*. It wasn't that the people were wrong, it's that the *match* for this chapter of the business had changed. Amplify starts when you stop hiring for what used to work and start designing for what the future needs. Let's connect the dots.

You've already reclaimed your leadership identity. You've already mapped the terrain. You're not guessing anymore, you're designing. So what now? Now it's time to look around the table and ask: **Who's coming with me? And do they even know how?** Because you can have the clearest strategy and the boldest direction… But if your people don't trust it, don't feel part of it, or don't believe they're safe to stretch toward it, nothing moves.

What you're really doing is this: You are not just managing roles. You're writing the emotional code your team will run on. If you lead with tension, they'll play it safe. If you lead with silence, they'll stay quiet too. If you lead with clarity, curiosity, and courage? They'll start borrowing that rhythm for themselves.

This is emotional intelligence in real-time, not as a buzzword, but as the difference between a team that delivers and a team that disappears into polite, passive resistance. And it goes deeper than tone. You also need to design the *shape* of the team that can carry your next chapter. That means asking hard, grown-up questions:

- Do you have the right people for where you're headed, not just where you've been?

- Are your "rockstars" aligned, or just familiar?

- Are your top performers also your culture amplifiers, or your silent culture killers?

As Trey Taylor writes in *A CEO Only Does Three Things*, it's not enough to have the right people in the right seats; "*they have to be facing the right direction, with their seatbelts off and sleeves rolled up.*" Your job isn't to create a perfect org chart. It's to build a *community of trust and traction*, people who stretch each other, challenge each other, and grow the thing with you.

This is where people-systems start to matter:

- 1-on-1s that aren't just status updates, but growth loops.

- Feedback that doesn't get buried under niceness.

- Recognition that reinforces the culture you're designing, not just who works the longest hours.

This is leadership design at the human layer, and it's not soft; it's structural.

You're Not Just Managing Roles, You're Building Belonging

You don't just lead projects. You lead humans. And the humans on your team? They don't move because of org charts. They move because of clarity, safety, ownership, and belief.

I know we've been calling them "soft skills" for decades. That's HR's favorite euphemism, like emotional intelligence is some bonus prize instead of the backbone of everything. But here's how I see it: These aren't soft skills, so knock that term out of your brain forever! They're core leadership skills, and no business survives without them. Because when your team doesn't feel seen, heard, trusted, or challenged? They check out. They coast. They nod in meetings and disappear in execution. You don't get innovation. You get inertia.

This is where leadership becomes human. Not coddling or cheerleading, but reading the room before it combusts. It's about knowing when someone's resistance is fear in disguise, and then choosing to grow the person, instead of just tracking the output. This is leadership design at the human layer, and if you ignore it, you'll spend the next year wondering why your smartest people quietly disengaged.

The Amplify swimlane is about the people who carry your culture, and whether your systems support them to rise or subtly tell them to shrink.

Systems: Process Is the Interface Between People and Progress

Let's talk systems. Not org charts. Not decks. Not your "strategic planning offsite" that turned into a 92-slide graveyard of good intentions. I mean the actual way work moves, or doesn't, through your team every day. Because here's the thing that often gets missed, even by seasoned leaders:

Your systems are the interface between your people and your progress.

If that interface is smooth, intuitive, and responsive, your people move with confidence. Decisions get made. Work flows. Momentum builds. But if that interface is clunky, outdated, or filled with friction, then everything slows down, alignment breaks, and your best people start spending more time working around the system than inside it. Sound familiar?

Maybe it's a sign-off process that takes six steps and four calendars to coordinate. Maybe it's a weekly meeting that's supposed to "drive alignment," but really just burns an hour with status updates no one listens to. Or maybe it's that old "collaboration tool" your team keeps pretending to use, while actually running the real work through backchannel texts and side chats.

Broken systems don't just waste time. They shape behavior.

They teach your team that effort doesn't matter. That clarity is optional. That progress is mostly about surviving the process, not solving the problem. And worst of all? You probably inherited most of them.

You didn't design these friction points; they just accumulated. A band-aid here. A workaround there. A workaround for the workaround when that didn't work. Then, all of a sudden, you wake up one day and realize: *I'm running a team of adults inside a system built for a haunted middle school group project.*

And yeah, I know that sounds harsh, but I've worked with too many brilliant leaders stuck in systems that treat grown, capable people like they need five approvals to move a paperclip.

Let's do better. Let's rebuild the interface. Let's turn systems into **trust engines**, not compliance machines.

Coach's Commentary

Systems either unlock your people or handcuff them.

The goal here isn't process for process's sake. It's clarity. It's speed. It's progress that doesn't require you personally being in every room. And when your systems run right? You don't just scale output. You scale leadership. This is what Amplify is about at the systems layer:

- Cutting friction

- Clarifying flow

- Designing tools and rituals that let your people win, without you hovering

And if you don't know where to start, just pick one process that drains your team's energy. One meeting, one workflow, one handoff. Then ask:

- What is this system *actually* rewarding?

- What is it slowing down?

- Who benefits, and who struggles?

If the answer makes you cringe, good. You've just found your next Amplify experiment.

In *Lean into Your Story*, you claimed the vision and clarified your direction. In *Empower Your Story*, you started designing systems of execution and trust. But here, in *Amplify*, you're shaping the environment that carries it all forward. Because leadership doesn't just live in your plans. It lives in how people feel, how systems behave, and how meaning is made, day after day

Core Experiments to Amplify Your Story

You don't amplify culture by preaching values. You amplify it by designing systems, shaping behavior, and building emotional signals that reinforce the story you want to live, not the one you're accidentally telling.

Every team carries cultural scar tissue, every system has drifted from its purpose, and every leader wrestles with how to develop people *while* delivering results. This is where we stop guessing and start designing. Each of the experiments below is a structural shift, targeted at the friction that's currently dragging your influence.

10 Sample Objectives in the Amplify Lane

Objectives in this lane are designed to amplify not just what you do, but how your team experiences your leadership. We broke down the three types back in Chapter 7 (and touched on them again in Chapter 8), so you already know the deal: some experiments stretch you, some shape your team, and some do both. The goal here isn't volume, it's traction. Pick one that moves the needle or design your own to meet the cultural signals and emotional dynamics you're actually navigating.

1. **Make Your Values Visible** *(Both)*. Move beyond slogans. Translate one core value into a ritual, decision-making norm, or behavior cue the team can see and follow.

2. **Uncover the Emotional Operating System** *(Team)*. Diagnose what feelings and unspoken fears are shaping decisions, collaboration, and risk tolerance on your team.

3. **Rebuild Trust After Cultural Drift** *(Team)*. Repair trust in a team that's been burned by past leadership, broken promises, or inconsistent feedback.

4. **Shift from Fear to Learning After Failure** *(Both).* Rewire how your team reacts to mistakes, moving from blame and silence to transparency and shared growth.

5. **Upgrade Feedback Loops** *(Both).* Transform feedback into a normal, useful rhythm rather than a scary, reactive event.

6. **Install a System for Recognition That Reinforces Culture** *(Team).* Align shoutouts and rewards with your actual values, not just hustle or heroics.

7. **Clean Up a Toxic Legacy Ritual** *(Both).* Replace an outdated or fear-reinforcing meeting, report, or system with one that builds clarity and trust.

8. **Codify Team Norms That Promote Belonging** *(Team).* Co-create a set of working agreements that help everyone understand what "good team behavior" looks like now.

9. **Run a Daily Emotional Clarity Pulse** *(Individual).* Pause for five minutes each morning to name your emotional state, energy level, and leadership intention. Track shifts over a week and reflect on what influenced your signal.

10. **Audit Your Leadership Energy Curve** *(Individual).* Log the moments each week where your energy surged or crashed. Use that data to adjust how you lead meetings, make decisions, or offer support.

Four Sample Experiments in the Amplify Lane

Each experiment below is labeled as **Individual**, **Team**, or **Both**, so you can decide whether it's designed for your own leadership development, your team's cultural evolution, or both. Pick one that matches your current context or use them as inspiration to create your own.

🔬 Experiment 1: Cultural Storytelling Audit

- **Type:** Team

- **Question/Problem:** What cultural story is my team operating from, and is it helping or hurting?

- **Hypothesis:** If I surface and reshape our cultural narratives, I can shift energy, clarity, and buy-in across the team.

- **Action Plan:** Identify one moment where the team's reaction feels driven by fear or past trauma. Ask, *What story are we telling ourselves about this change?* Rewrite it with your team's help. Embed the new story in how you open meetings or frame priorities.

- **Timeframe:** 30 days

- **Measure:** Change in team tone, energy, or participation when referencing the new narrative. Track reactions in three or more team touchpoints.

- **Reflection:** What old stories were running the show? Did rewriting the narrative shift how the team responded? What stories now deserve airtime?

🔬 Experiment 2: Transformative 1-on-1s

- **Type:** Both

- **Question/Problem:** Are my 1-on-1s driving growth, or just checking boxes?

- **Hypothesis:** If I run coaching-style 1-on-1s for 30 days, I'll deepen trust and see more initiative from my team.

- **Action Plan:** Block 30 days of 1-on-1s. Use the same format each time: Start with a growth question, reflect on a stretch goal, and end with one forward action. Capture reflections along the way.

- **Timeframe:** 30 days

- **Measure:** Evidence of increased ownership, trust, or initiative in team members (e.g., stretch moves, honest feedback, self-directed wins).

- **Reflection:** What changed when you stopped talking status and started talking stretch? Which team members rose? What should your new 1-on-1 ritual be?

🔬 Experiment 3: Process Sunset

- **Type:** Team

- **Question/Problem:** What outdated system is draining our energy or sending the wrong cultural signal?

- **Hypothesis:** If I eliminate one obsolete process and replace it with a simple, strategic one, we'll unlock flow and reduce friction.

- **Action Plan:** Identify a process that causes confusion, duplicative work, or fear. Redesign it with your team. Replace it with a lightweight ritual that aligns with current priorities. Run it for 30 days.

- **Timeframe:** 30 days

- **Measure:** Compare friction (time delays, misunderstandings, rework) before and after. Gather team input on clarity and energy.

- **Reflection:** What legacy habits were holding the team back? What's possible now that the friction is gone? What else needs a sunset?

🔬 Experiment 4: Conflict Clarity Check

- **Type:** Individual

- **Question/Problem:** Am I modeling healthy conflict, or quietly avoiding the hard stuff?

- **Hypothesis:** If I name tension directly and frame it as collaboration, I'll lower defensiveness and increase trust.

- **Action Plan:** Identify one recurring point of tension. Use a structured script (e.g., "I noticed X, I'm wondering about Y, and I'd like to explore Z") to surface it constructively. Run this once a week for 30 days in different contexts.

- **Measure:** Outcomes of the conversations, more movement, less triangulation, clearer commitments.

- **Reflection:** What changed in the tone or trust of your relationships? What's your new go-to move for defusing conflict with clarity?

Want more experiments in this lane? There's a full Amplify Experiment Library waiting in the back of the book, covering culture, emotional intelligence, and system design with bite-sized moves you can test inside your team.

You Don't Just Work in Culture, You Work Through It

You don't need a louder message. You need a stronger signal. That's what *Amplify* is all about. Not charisma. Not communication theater. But repeatable signals, encoded in how you show up, how your systems move, and how your people feel when they work with you.

Culture doesn't hang on a wall. It gets architected by the systems you shape, the rhythms you protect, and the signals you send without even realizing it. This is Rung 5 & 6 work. And your leadership? It either reinforces the default or rewrites it. It doesn't live in your decks, your meetings, or your Slack threads. It lives in the unspoken playbook your team follows when you're not in the room.

- Your **systems** either unlock progress or grind your people down.

- Your **people** either stretch because of your presence or shrink because of your silence.

- Your **culture** either amplifies your message or edits it out of fear.

If you want long-term traction, you need an environment that runs the clarity without you constantly propping it up. That means:

- Emotional systems your team can breathe in,

- Structural systems they can move through,

- Cultural signals they can believe in.

That's what you're building now. That's *Amplify*.

Driving Question

- What's one invisible system or emotional rule shaping your team right now, and is it helping you scale or stall?

Your Coaching Question From Jim

If I dropped in anonymously and asked your team, "What's it like to work here?" what would they say?

Now, what do you *wish* they would say, and what's one leadership move you could make this month to pull those two answers closer together?

Mini Challenge: The Culture Pulse Cycle

✍ Download Worksheet: W9 – Culture Pulse + Influence Audit

Pick one cultural touchpoint: a meeting, a ritual, a system that seems "harmless." Then ask yourself:

- What signal is this sending?

- What story is it reinforcing?

- What's the hidden fear or default this is protecting?

Then run a two-week micro-experiment:

- Change the ritual.

- Adjust the format.

- Rewrite the script.

- Make the invisible visible.

After two weeks, debrief:

- What shifted?

- What stayed stuck?

- What surprised you?

Culture doesn't shift in slogans. It shifts in systems, in signals, and in what you repeat when no one's watching.

Final Reframe: Culture Is the Operating System, And You're the Architect

☞ If you remember nothing else from this chapter, remember this:

You don't just operate inside a culture. You operate through it.

And that culture decides whether your ideas move or quietly die in a folder somewhere.

Your real legacy isn't the last strategy you presented. It's the rhythm, resilience, and clarity your people carry forward when your name's no longer on the slide. If you want to lead like a CEO, you have to act like a systems architect. You need to be someone who shapes trust, clarity, and ownership by design. Because when the projects fade and the meetings stop, what lasts is how your leadership made people feel and what you made possible. That's where we're headed next.

CHAPTER 10

Be Remembered for the Right Reasons

Burnout isn't a badge of honor.
It's a warning sign that your systems are broken.

– Jim Saliba

You've heard it before: "You need more executive presence."

But what does that actually mean? It's tossed around like corporate cologne; everyone smells it, but no one can define it. This chapter is where we stop guessing.

Durability, the fourth lane of the **L.E.A.D. Laboratory**, isn't about polish, perfection, or pretending. It's about clarity, courage, and consistency, especially when the pressure rises. Not once. Not when it's convenient. Every single day.

Durable leaders aren't remembered for a standout presentation. They're remembered for how they show up when it's hard. They stay sharp when others spin. They stay grounded when the room tilts. Their presence becomes a form of trust, earned not through flash but through rhythm.

In the pages ahead, we'll build that kind of presence through three essential layers:

- **Presence.** How you show up when stakes are high and what people come to rely on.

- **Brand.** The reputation your leadership earns over time, and the perception gap that might be standing in the way.

- **Balance.** The systems that let you last, while others sprint straight into exhaustion.

Durability doesn't begin when you get promoted. It starts the moment your leadership becomes steady enough for others to lean on. Not when it's easy, but when it's needed most.

The Myth We're Breaking: "Executive Presence Means Being Polished and Perfect"

Sure, if your goal is to land a cameo in a painfully awkward corporate training video, then appearing perfect could work for you. But if you're actually leading? That kind of polish won't get you very far. Presence has less to do with how crisp your blazer is and more to do with what people feel from you when things go sideways.

The myth says presence is about looking the part. Clean slides and a measured tone. No sweat, no stumbles, just smooth delivery and practiced lines. But here's what people are really asking for when they say, "You need more executive presence." What they actually mean is:

"Make me feel better about following you when things get messy."

That's not a dig. It's a fair request because presence isn't how you perform. It's how you hold the room when the ground shifts. It's what people read in your face when the deal tanks, when the board pushes back, when the answer is "I don't know yet."

If your team only trusts you when you've rehearsed, that's not presence; that's performance. You don't need to be the most impressive voice in the room. But you do need to be the one people instinctively look toward when the pressure rises. You need to be steady, composed, and clear enough that other people can breathe.

So, the next time someone tells you to "work on your executive presence," don't translate that as "be more impressive." Translate it as: Can people anchor to you when it's hard?

If not, that's the work you need to do.

The Pain Behind It

Leaders don't fall apart because they lack talent. They fall apart because they've been trained to perform instead of lead. They spend so much energy trying to look composed, polished, positive, and prepared that they forget to build the internal rhythm that actually keeps them steady. And eventually, it catches up with them, because underneath that performance is not just pressure, but fear. Fear of being seen as unsure. Fear of getting it wrong. Fear of vulnerability dressed up as professionalism. What starts as confidence becomes compensation. What started as "putting your best foot forward" becomes a full-time performance. Until suddenly, even your team can feel the gap between the version of you in the all-hands and the version of you in the 4:00 p.m. debrief after things went sideways.

That gap doesn't just cost credibility. It costs trust.

Presence doesn't come from perfect prep. It comes from emotional consistency, especially when the heat is on. If you crack every time the stakes rise, your team will feel it, even if they never say it.

This is how burnout creeps in. Not from too much work, but from the exhausting effort of constantly managing how you're perceived. You're not just leading. You're editing, polishing, and performing, all while slowly losing the capacity to just be present.

You don't need to be fearless. But you do need to be stable enough that people can trust you'll still be standing when things get shaky. That's the heart of executive presence: not showmanship, but **signal strength**. Not the ability to impress, but the capacity to hold weight without transferring it to everyone else. And when you don't build that muscle? The pressure doesn't disappear. It just shifts onto your team.

Michael: From Control to Clarity

You first met Michael back in Chapter 2, the sharp, capable leader whose default mode was to fill the void and keep the wheels turning. By Chapter 8, he had started shifting from reactive helper to intentional owner. But there was still a piece missing: presence.

Not performance. Presence.

In meetings, Michael came across as buttoned-up and prepared. Polished and professional, but also… unreadable.

After a high-stakes planning session where a project had slipped again, his boss looked him in the eye and said, "I need to know you've got this." Michael nodded, kept his voice even, and said all the right things.

But something didn't land. He thought he was projecting calm. What actually came through was indifference.

In our next session, I asked, "What do you think your team picks up from you when things go sideways?"

He paused. "Probably nothing. I try to stay professional and keep it together, not add fuel."

Then he added, "I'm not hiding… but I'm definitely managing what I show."

That's the irony. You work so hard to stay composed that you stop showing up at all. Michael wasn't giving his team anything to anchor to. There was no urgency, no emotional signal, no sense of support, just silence and motion. And that absence told a story of its own:

"This must not be that important."

Presence isn't about raising your voice. It's about making your leadership legible. We didn't need Michael to speak more. We needed him to show up in a way his team could read and rally behind, even when he wasn't spelling it out.

Coach's Commentary

If your team is filling in the blanks, you're not leading with presence; you're leading with ambiguity.

The Five Dimensions of Executive Presence

Executive presence isn't charisma. It's not a "vibe." And it's definitely not how polished you look in a pitch deck.

When I coach leaders on presence, I don't hand them a checklist. I walk them through five core dimensions. These are the anchors. When they're strong, people trust you more. When they're inconsistent, people hesitate, even if you're competent. Here's how I break it down for clients:

1. Identification

Do you actually know what you stand for, and is that where you lead from when it matters?

This ties directly back to Step 1 of the Six-Step Leadership Challenge: Introspection. You clarified your leadership identity there. Now the question is: do you *still* anchor to it under pressure? If your values vanish the moment tension rises, you haven't built a compass; you've built camouflage, and without a compass, every decision feels heavier, every challenge more chaotic.

This was Michael's gap. He wasn't doing anything wrong, but he wasn't leading from anything clear. His choices weren't grounded in visible principles, so when pressure hit, he defaulted to performance. His team didn't know what he stood for because, in the toughest moments, he wasn't sure either.

2. Presentation

How do people experience you in the moments that matter?

This isn't about communication style, it's about presence when it counts. It's how you carry yourself in meetings, in conflict, in everyday interactions. Do people see someone steady, grounded, and trustworthy, or do they get tension, vagueness, and discomfort, especially when things go sideways?

Presentation is where **extrospection** shows up. Back in Step 2, you started reading the room. Now it's about understanding what the room reads *from you*.

Michael's signal broke down here. His presentation was too neutral, too controlled, too polished, and too quiet. It read as distant. People didn't get urgency or confidence from him. They just got empty space. And in a leadership environment, empty space gets filled with doubt, delay, or indecision.

3. Communication

Can you make people feel smarter for being in the room with you?

Communication isn't just about clarity, it's about effect. Can people follow your thinking? Do they leave the conversation more confident, more focused, or just more confused? This isn't about being the most articulate speaker. It's about removing friction from the signal. Leaders with strong communication presence don't just explain things. They *land* them.

You don't need to dumb it down. But you do need to get to the point, particularly in critical moments. You don't build trust with long-winded answers and hedge language. You build it by helping people understand what matters and what happens next.

Back in Step 3, you drafted a vision worth leading toward. Communication is how that vision moves through the organization. It's how people pick it up, carry it forward, and act on it. If they can't repeat what you just said without rereading the slide, it's not presence, it's noise.

4. Affiliation

Who's around you, and what do they amplify?

This isn't about having the right connections. It's about having the right voices in your ear. The people closest to you, your team, your boss, your peers, even those informal advisors, shape how you think, how you lead, and how you're perceived.

And it's not just one direction. Affiliation runs up, down, and side to side.

I often ask my clients: "Who's filling your sails, and who's quietly anchoring you to the dock?" That question alone reveals a lot about why someone's presence feels sharp… or stuck.

Back in Chapter 8, we talked about building a team that thinks without you. This is the next layer: building a network that not only executes but also **elevates**. Because presence isn't created in isolation, it's shaped through proximity.

And proximity isn't limited to your org chart. Your presence is also shaped by the world you engage with (or avoid). Are you part of a broader professional network? Do you seek out perspectives beyond your function, your industry, or your bubble? The leaders who grow tend to stay in motion, both inside *and* outside the building.

Your brand doesn't just come from what you say. It comes from who sees you lead, and what they say when you're not in the room.

5. Action

Do you follow through, especially when no one's watching?

This is the trust layer. You can talk a good game and show up well in meetings, but if you don't deliver consistently, your presence won't last. It'll erode every time your behavior fails to back up your message.

Presence without action is theater. Presence with action is leadership.

In Step 5, we will build feedback loops and action rhythms into your leadership operating system. This is the daily version: Do your words match your behavior, not once, but every time?

Michael had strong follow-through. That wasn't his issue. But without clarity in identification or presentation, that follow-through wasn't reinforcing presence, it was just keeping things moving quietly in the background.

Consistency builds reputation. Visibility gives it weight. If people can count on you to follow through when things get hard, they won't need to overanalyze what you say. They'll just believe you.

Leadership Brand and the Presence Gap

Let's talk about your leadership brand. Not the aspirational list on your LinkedIn profile. The one that actually lives in people's heads, the version of you they describe when you're not in the room to explain yourself. Don't let your brand build itself passively, between meetings and in the gaps between decisions. Don't assume that good work just speaks for itself.

The Presence Gap Map

Before you assume your presence is landing the way you intend, pause. There's often a gap between what you *think* you're signaling and what people are actually picking up. I call this the **Presence Gap**, and it's where a lot of good leaders stall.

You think you're coming across as focused, but they see you as cold. You think you're being steady, but they see you as detached. You think you're building confidence, but they're still waiting for clarity.

This disconnect doesn't always show up in feedback forms. It shows up in hesitation. In missed opportunities. In that weird silence after you say something important, and no one moves.

The map is simple:

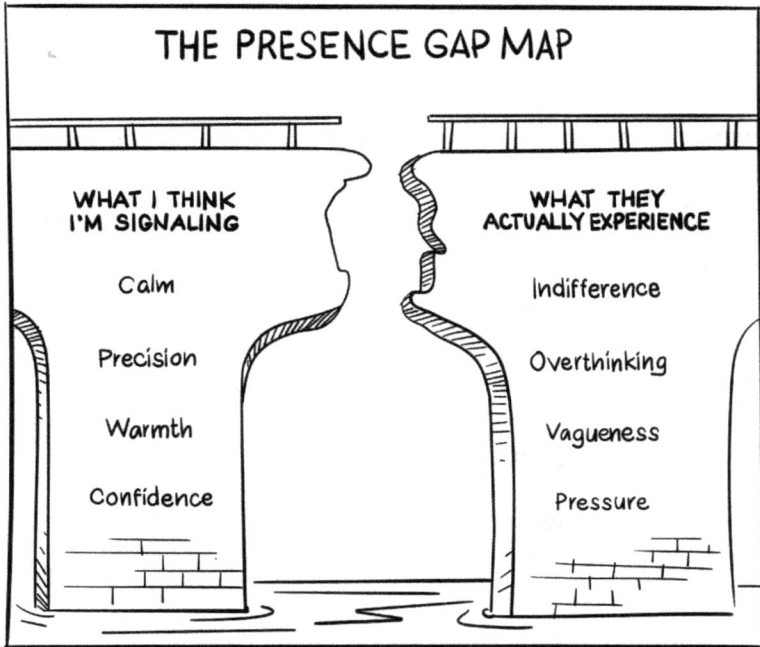

THE PRESENCE GAP MAP

WHAT I THINK I'M SIGNALING

Calm

Precision

Warmth

Confidence

WHAT THEY ACTUALLY EXPERIENCE

Indifference

Overthinking

Vagueness

Pressure

That's why presence isn't just about style, it's about perception. You don't get to decide what your presence *is*. You get to decide what you *build*. The rest is in the hands of the people who experience it.

The Brand Backward Test

If you want to know how your leadership is being experienced, stop asking for feedback on your *performance*. Ask about your *impression*. Here's the simplest test I use with clients:

Ask three people across various levels of your org to describe your leadership in three adjectives. Don't explain. Don't overthink it. Just ask. Then write down the three words you want to be known for.

Compare the two lists.

If they match, great! Now make it consistent. If they don't, you've just found your blind spot.

This isn't a branding exercise. It's a leadership reality check. Your *real* brand is your presence, and if you're not shaping it with intention, you're leaving it to everyone else's worst day.

You see, leadership isn't self-explanatory. If people have to guess what kind of leader you are, they'll either fill in the blanks or stop paying attention altogether. This is where I ask clients two simple questions:

- If your team had to describe your leadership in three words, what would they say?

- Now… what do you *wish* they'd say?

That gap? That's your next development move. And yes, we all have one. That's not a flaw, it's the work. Great leaders aren't just consistent in how they show up. They're intentional about how they're remembered.

Tonya's Brand Shift

Tonya, a sharp, strategic acting COO at a fast-scaling manufacturing and tech company, has been in your orbit since the early chapters. From the start, she delivered, her ops were clean, and her team respected her. If something broke, she fixed it, fast.

Earlier in this journey, she ran a simple five-minute experiment: in a key meeting, instead of just reporting status, she presented trade-off options and made a clear recommendation. It was small, but it shifted something. People listened differently. She felt the room lean in.

That was the spark.

Now, months later, the patterns are bigger, but the shift is the same.

Tonya had started to notice that while she was trusted to *run* the ship, she still wasn't being invited to *steer* it. She wasn't being pulled into early strategy sessions or asked to weigh in on directional bets. She wasn't missing goals. She was missing presence.

In one of our sessions, I asked her, "What story are you telling that shows you can shape what comes next?"

She paused. "I don't think I've been telling one. I've just been... delivering."

That was the turn. It wasn't about polish, but about positioning.

Tonya realized her brand was competent, calm, and reliable, but not catalytic. That early experiment gave her a blueprint. She didn't need a rebrand. She needed to scale what was already working. So, she kept going:

- Instead of just surfacing operational risks, she framed them within strategic narratives.

- Instead of waiting for assignments, she brought forward options and directional trade-offs.

- Instead of just proving she could hold the present, she started signaling she could shape the future.

Slowly, the perception shifted. She didn't campaign for a seat at the table. She showed up like someone who already belonged there, because presence isn't about volume, it's about intention. Tonya stopped waiting to be noticed and started leading in a way that couldn't be missed.

Coach's Commentary

You don't earn leadership presence by being useful. You earn it by showing people you can see what's next and move them toward it.

Life Balance Is a Leadership Strategy

If you're killing it at work but collapsing at home, or the reverse, you're not winning. You're leaking durability. Your leadership isn't just about stamina. It's about sustainability. If your systems only work when you're running hot, they're broken by design.

You can't show up with presence, clarity, or calm if you're constantly running on fumes. Eventually, your tone frays, your signal drops, and your team starts to feel it, even if they can't name it.

Durability means showing up sharp, not just showing up. It means protecting your energy like a strategic asset, not treating it like an unlimited tap. That requires boundaries, rhythms, and recovery, not just willpower.

I often ask clients, "How do you recharge, and how often?" The most common response?

Silence.

Then maybe: "Well, I used to…" or "I guess I don't really."

That tells me everything, because burnout doesn't usually announce itself. It builds quietly through over-commitment, over-functioning, and constantly performing at the cost of your own capacity.

I once worked with a CEO who was all about the numbers. He tracked every metric, drove his team hard, and kept the company performing quarter after quarter. From the outside, it looked like it was working. Then, one night, his wife sat him down and said, "You're never here. And even when you are, you're not really. I don't know how much more I can take."

That was the moment. Not a missed target. Not a board conversation. A personal wake-up call that his leadership, however effective on paper, was costing more than it was worth.

Balance doesn't mean everything gets equal time. It means your leadership doesn't cost you more than you're willing to pay. And yes, your team is watching. They notice when you glorify the grind and disappear on weekends. They notice when you say "We value balance," but don't model it. They notice when you show up exhausted and call it dedication.

If you want to lead in a way that lasts, you need more than vision and execution. You need a life that can support your leadership because if it only works when you're running on empty, it doesn't actually work.

Routines That Sustain You

Durability doesn't live in your inbox or in your heroic "just one more late night" mode. It lives in your routines. If you're relying on willpower to stay consistent, you're already behind because willpower fades. Routines don't.

Durable leaders aren't just resilient. They're intentional. They build rhythms that reinforce the kind of presence they want to show up with and routines that anchor their clarity, protect their energy, and keep their leadership from burning out under its own expectations. That includes:

- Weekly rhythms that keep you anchored, not reactive.

- Personal rituals that reconnect you to purpose, not just performance.

- Feedback loops that keep you learning without spiraling.

- Recovery practices that treat energy like fuel, not an afterthought.

You don't need a 17-step planner and a stack of wellness hacks. You need one or two routines that you protect consistently, the ones that help you move with focus when everything else feels noisy. Skip these routines, and you're signing up for chaos on repeat.

Want to know if you're building sustainable leadership? Look at your calendar and your habits, and then ask: Are these making me clearer, or just keeping me busy?

> ## Coach's Commentary
>
> Sustainable leadership isn't about doing less. It's about doing what actually supports your signal.

10 Sample Objectives in the Durability Lane

Durability isn't a personality trait. It's a design.

This lane is about showing up in a way that holds steady in challenging moments through transition, and across time. That kind of leadership doesn't come from talent. It comes from clarity, systems, and consistency.

If you want to build presence that lasts, you don't need to do more. You need to **design smarter**. Each of the objectives below targets a different layer of durable leadership and gives you a 30-day focus to practice and refine it.

10 Objectives for the Durability Lane

Just like in earlier chapters, each objective is labeled Individual, Team, or Both, depending on whether it's designed to strengthen your own durable leadership habits, boost your team's resilience, or do both at once. Use the ones that create real traction, or design your own to match your role, rhythms, and reality.

1. **Signal Steadiness in High-Stakes Moments** *(Both)*. Help your team feel anchored when pressure spikes. Practice visible steadiness, through posture, tone, and framing, in one recurring high-stakes meeting each week.

2. **Build a Repeatable End-of-Week Recharge** *(Individual)*. Energy isn't infinite, so make recovery a ritual. Test a weekly rhythm: Friday afternoon reflection, a reset habit (walk, journaling, calendar cleanup, or strategy pulse), and one visible reset action.

3. **Practice Being Seen, Not Just Effective** *(Individual)*. Competence isn't enough if no one knows how you think. Choose one meeting each week to share not just what you decided, but how you got there. Make your reasoning visible.

4. **Close the Brand Gap With One Shift** *(Individual)*. Small signal mismatches create major disconnects. Ask three peers to describe your leadership in three words. Choose one behavior to shift each week that better aligns with your intended brand.

5. **Make Clarity Your Default, Not a Surprise** *(Both)*. People can't follow if they're always guessing. Before each key message or meeting, set a one-sentence intent: what you want people to feel, know, and do. Debrief afterward to assess the gap.

6. **Protect One Hour a Week Like It's Gold** *(Individual)*. Durable leadership requires strategic solitude. Block one hour every week as a non-negotiable space for reflection, thinking, or proactive planning. Defend it like it matters.

7. **Shrink the Recovery Window After Setbacks** *(Individual)*. It's not about avoiding stress. It's about rebounding faster. After any tough moment, ask: What cracked? What held? What will I do differently next time? Make this part of your weekly rhythm.

8. **Lead With Intentional Warmth in Uncertain Moments** *(Both)*. People don't need perfection. They need stability with humanity. Practice visible empathy during change, conflict, or ambiguity by acknowledging what's real and re-anchoring to direction.

9. **Normalize Energy Conversations** *(Team)*. Exhaustion is a system signal, not a personal flaw. Introduce energy check-ins at the end of key meetings: What fueled you? What drained you? What shift would help next time?

10. **Build Your Brand Sentence and Test It Weekly** *(Individual).*
Be known for what you stand for, not just what you do. Craft a single sentence that defines the leadership presence you want to be known for. Each week, ask yourself: Did I lead in alignment with that sentence?

These aren't vague platitudes about "being more present." They're real-world tests. Below are three core experiments designed to stretch your presence, sharpen your brand, and protect your leadership energy, because durable leaders don't wait to fall apart before they build their foundations.

🔬 Experiment 1: Presence Playback

- **Type:** Individual

- **Question/Problem:** Do I show up with a steady, readable presence when the pressure rises?

- **Hypothesis:** If I watch myself in high-stakes meetings and reflect weekly, I'll discover where my presence is helping, or hindering, my impact.

- **Action Plan:** Record one key meeting each week for 30 days. Watch without sound to observe body language, tone, and clarity. Journal one insight per review and track shifts over time.

- **Timeframe:** 30 days

- **Measure:** Number of presence shifts or habits identified. Feedback from peers on signal clarity. Personal confidence in high-pressure settings.

- **Reflection:** What signal do I send before I speak? What's working, and what's missing? What new habits are helping me anchor the room?

🔬 Experiment 2: The Brand Backwards Test

- **Type:** Individual

- **Question/Problem:** Is there a gap between how I want to be seen and how people actually experience me?

- **Hypothesis:** If I ask others for their impression of my leadership, I'll spot branding blind spots and adjust my behavior with intent.

- **Action Plan:** Ask three people across levels to describe your leadership in three words. Write down the three words you want to be known for. Identify one behavior that reinforces the wrong story. Shift it each week.

- **Timeframe:** 30 days

- **Measure:** Alignment between original and desired brand words. Peer feedback on visibility and consistency. Personal clarity and confidence.

- **Reflection:** What surprised me about the words others chose? What am I projecting unintentionally? What shift had the biggest impact?

🔬 Experiment 3: The Non-Negotiable Hour

- **Type:** Individual

- **Question/Problem:** Am I protecting my energy and reflection time, or just reacting all week?

- **Hypothesis:** If I block and protect one hour a week for strategic recharge, I'll show up with sharper thinking and more sustainable presence.

- **Action Plan:** Choose one hour each week. Label it "Non-Negotiable" on your calendar. Use it for reflection, thinking, or personal clarity, not catch-up work. Reflect weekly on what it gave you.

- **Timeframe:** 30 days

- **Measure:** Consistency of protected time. Shifts in clarity, energy, and strategic focus. Team perception of your steadiness.

- **Reflection:** What changed when I carved out time for myself? What did that space make possible? What boundaries helped me protect it?

Want to Go Further?

There's a full library of durability experiments waiting in the back of the book. These include tools to map your stress signals, audit your brand shadow, and build feedback loops that protect your energy without losing momentum.

You'll find them in the companion resources, but feel free to reach out if you want to run them live with coaching and feedback.

Driving Question

- If your leadership had to speak for you, no titles, no résumé, just the ripple effect you leave behind, what would it say? If that imprint isn't quite the one you want to leave behind, this is where you start reshaping it.

Your Coaching Question From Jim

At the end of each week for the next month, ask yourself:

- Did I lead in a way that's worth remembering?

- Where was I clear, and where was I cloudy?

- Where did I model resilience, and where did I just muscle through?

Write down one move you're proud of, and one you want to shift.

Remember: Durable leadership isn't what you *preach*. It's what you *repeat*, especially when no one's watching.

Mini Challenge: Build Your Leadership Brand Cycle

Download Worksheet: W10 – Brand Builder + Presence Lab

This week, run a simple but sharp presence audit:

1. **Identify three high-visibility moments**, such as meetings, decisions, or conversations, where your presence will matter.

2. **Set one sentence of intent** for each. (Example: "I will show up with clarity and calm, not caveats.")

3. **Reflect after each one.** Did I match my intention, or miss it?

4. **At the end of the week, write your leadership brand in one sentence.**

Now ask: Is it the brand you want? If not, what's one shift you'll make next week to close the gap? Because presence is what you practice. And your story is being written, whether you're intentional about it or not.

Final Reframe

Durability Is the Quiet Power That Outlasts Noise

You won't be remembered for how busy you were. You'll be remembered for how steady you were, how you showed up, how you made people feel, and how you carried weight, especially when the ground shook. You see, you don't build executive presence by trying to impress people. You build it by becoming someone people can trust to hold steady, day after day, when it matters most.

If you forget everything else from this chapter, remember this:

Presence isn't a performance. It's a pattern.

The more consistent you are, especially when it's hard, the more durable your leadership becomes. You want to lead like a CEO? Then start acting like the architect of your presence now, not later.

In the next chapter, we're not just talking about being durable. We're going to put all of it into motion and show you what it looks like to lead through feedback, iteration, and real-world adaptation. Chapter 11 is where we tighten the loop by building routines that can adapt in real-world conditions and keep momentum moving forward. It's where we test everything you've built and prove that your leadership doesn't just hold, it evolves.

CHAPTER 11

Action + Reaction = The 30-Day Flywheel

Momentum doesn't come from the perfect plan.
It comes from moving before you're ready.

– Jim Saliba

Everyone's got a plan until the real world punches it in the mouth. Plenty of leaders can design a "perfect" 90-day roadmap. Then they act surprised when reality doesn't follow the blueprint. It never does.

You don't need a plan that looks good on paper. You need a system that survives contact with chaos and evolves while you're in motion. Resilience isn't just about bouncing back after you get wrecked. It's about bending without breaking and building your next move while the last one's still catching heat. Leadership isn't about launching the perfect test and hoping it sticks. It's about running the test, reading the punch, and pivoting fast enough to stay dangerous.

This is Step 5 of the Six-Step Leadership Challenge: Action + Reaction. You've built the plan. Now it's time to run it, learn from it, and adapt fast, not by gritting your teeth and powering through, but by sharpening your reflexes as you go. You already know your 90-day plan won't run on autopilot. This phase is about staying sharp, staying flexible, and actually learning while you're moving. Leadership resilience doesn't come from the plan. It comes from how you lead when the plan starts leaking mid-flight.

The Structure: Vision, Milestones, Goals, Experiments

Before you build your first flywheel, you need a structure that doesn't collapse the second things get loud. Back in Chapter 7, we already cleaned up the strategy buzzword mess: vision, goals, strategy, tactics, all the terms people love to use interchangeably, like that makes them sound smart. It doesn't. It makes them sound lost.

So, here's the reminder, because we're about to actually use that structure. If you skipped Chapter 7, that was a bad call. Go fix it.

You start with your 12-month vision. Not a corporate slogan. Not some vague "empower the team" fluff. A clear, specific picture of what leadership looks like when you're doing it right, one year from now. Your systems are humming. You're not the go-to firefighter anymore.

You've got a team that moves without panic, a calendar that reflects your priorities, and a leadership presence that doesn't rely on jumping into every problem with a superhero cape.

Now you break that vision down into four quarterly milestones. These aren't checkboxes. They're real shifts. If you want to get to that vision, these are the chunks of ground you have to cover. Think of them like strategic stepping stones, not the usual "Q2: Improve synergy" nonsense.

Each milestone becomes the basis for your 90-day L.E.A.D. goals. One goal per swimlane: Lean, Empower, Amplify, and Durability. This is where we get focused. What's the strategic spine you need to clarify? What systems need to run without you? What cultural story are you reinforcing? And how are you showing up as a leader who doesn't spike cortisol every time there's a Slack alert?

Now we set the 30-60-90 day objectives that move each goal forward. You don't need to fill in every box like it's a group project. You focus where the leverage is.

Then the good stuff, experiments. These are not "tasks." These are small, smart tests designed to learn fast and lead faster. Each one starts with a hypothesis, has a time limit, and comes with a scoreboard. If it works, great! Scale it. If it stumbles, refine it. If it dies, toss it and move on. No drama. No PowerPoint postmortems. Just learn while you lead.

The structure is simple:

1. Vision

2. Milestones

3. L.E.A.D. goals

4. Objectives

5. Experiments

If you mix those up, you end up spinning in circles, but if you build them in order, you'll get traction that holds even when conditions change. Not theory. Not wishful thinking. Real leadership, moving forward, one flywheel at a time.

David's 90-Day L.E.A.D. Laboratory

Let's bring this thing to life with David, who was tired of pretending his quarterly roadmap reviews were anything more than theater. He has a real vision: Twelve months from now, he wants his tech org running with speed, clarity, and actual leverage. Not PowerPoints. Not noise. Traction.

The vision was sharp: two strategic initiatives launched and delivering, senior leaders stepping up, a weekly rhythm that connects tech work to business results, and David not being the bottleneck, but designing systems that scale without him constantly playing traffic cop.

That's the destination. Now comes the build.

So let's take a look at the whole arc. David's not just chasing quarterly wins. He's building toward a long-term shift in how his org operates, how it moves, collaborates, and scales. Here's how we mapped it:

David's 12-Month Vision

Twelve months from now, David isn't holding the reins of every decision. He's built a tech organization that leads with confidence, clarity, and velocity. His team moves with purpose, not waiting for permission. Strategy is no longer a presentation; it's embedded in the rhythm of the work. Senior leaders are driving meaningful change without handholding. The org isn't just aligned; it's energized, trusted by the business, and positioned as a driver of competitive edge. David's influence lives in the systems, the culture, and the leaders he's grown, so progress continues even when he's not in the room.

To get there, we broke the vision into four quarterly milestones.

Q1: Launch Two Cross-Functional Bets From the Tech Roadmap

This quarter pressure-tests the team's ability to collaborate across silos without defaulting back to David. It's not about the deliverables; it's about shared ownership. If these bets gain traction without David quarterbacking every meeting, it proves the organization can move with horizontal muscle, not just vertical hierarchy. Success here lays the groundwork for trust, autonomy, and scaled execution.

Q2: Install a Visible Strategy Spine and Execution Rhythm

This milestone is about making strategy operational. David builds the scaffolding that turns ambition into weekly action. A clear strategy spine connects big-picture goals to day-to-day work. Shared rhythms create predictability and signal what matters. When the system runs smoothly without fire drills or babysitting, the team starts to breathe and accelerate.

Q3: Empower Two Direct Reports to Run Their Own Experiments

This is where David stops being the center of gravity. Two of his leaders take the reins, running their own bets, making high-leverage decisions, and managing risk. It's not just about delegation, it's about trust, capability, and momentum. This quarter tests whether David can build real leadership capacity beneath him so influence isn't centralized and progress doesn't stall when he's out of the room.

Q4: Systematize Durable Leadership Habits Across the Org

By Q4, the habits built through experimentation become part of the organization's DNA. Strategic cycles, coaching loops, and feedback rituals aren't just experiments; they're how the org operates. David installs infrastructure that protects leadership durability long after the coaching ends. This quarter proves that what started as personal growth has scaled into cultural transformation.

Each milestone builds on the last. You see, there's no leapfrogging. There's no skipping to the "install culture" part if you haven't built ownership or rhythm yet. These milestones don't just track progress. They sequence transformation.

Now let's zero in on Q1 and watch how David turned that milestone into movement using three 30-day flywheels, stacked for momentum, each one stretching the team without snapping the system. For Q1, David picked this:

Launch two cross-functional bets from the tech roadmap.

Sounds simple, right? Kick off two initiatives. But we weren't testing whether he could start projects. We were testing whether his org could collaborate across silos without falling apart the second he stepped back. That's the real game. So, we reframed the milestone:

Pilot a new model of cross-functional collaboration by launching two tech-led bets that clarify shared goals, enable co-ownership, and model what strategic partnership, not just support, looks like.

That reframing changed the work. Now it wasn't just about launching. It was about leadership habits, team dynamics, and cultural friction.

From there, we built his 90-day plan using the L.E.A.D. swimlanes: Lean (strategy), Empower (ownership), Amplify (culture), Durability (presence). In this arc, each lane carried an added layer to match the real work ahead:

- Lean focused on **strategy plus focus.**

- Empower zeroed in on **ownership plus systems.**

- Amplify elevated **culture plus influence.**

- Durability reinforced **presence plus sustainability.**

And no, we didn't fill every box. That's a rookie mistake. David focused his effort where it mattered most. It wasn't about doing it all; it was about making it effective.

LEAN (Strategy + Focus)

Q1 Goal: Launch 2 cross-functional bets with a clear strategic spine and visible traction.

Month 1

- Objective: Draft and test one-pagers (Strategy Spines) for each bet

- Experiment: Build the drafts, then run feedback loops with two peer execs

- Measure: Can they clearly explain the bet's purpose and strategic value?

Month 2

- Objective: Socialize the bets across functions

- Experiment: Host alignment sessions with the GMs

- Measure: Agreement on next steps, and whether pushback shows up early

Month 3? Empty. On purpose. He front-loaded the energy here to get momentum early.

EMPOWER (Ownership + Systems)

Q1 Goal: Build ownership structures so the bets don't bottleneck at David.

Month 2

- **Objective:** Map decision rights

- **Experiment:** Use the Role Clarifier Canvas with each initiative lead

- **Measure:** Number of lingering clarification requests and lead confidence pulse

Month 3

- **Objective:** Run a Delegation Sprint

- **Experiment:** Define decision boundaries, set a support rhythm, then back off

- **Measure:** Decision speed and lead's confidence score

This lane wasn't about perfect org charts. It was about pressure-testing ownership.

AMPLIFY (Culture + Influence)

Q1 Goal: Reinforce a culture of shared authorship and visibility.

Month 2

- **Objective:** Make early wins visible

- **Experiment:** Share one initiative story in three places (email, meeting, Slack)

- **Measure:** Peer reactions, engagement, and echoing from other leaders

Month 3

- **Objective:** Build a ritual for learning

- **Experiment:** Launch a "Win, Learn, Next" moment in team standups

- **Measure:** Participation rate and signs that it spreads without him pushing it

Culture doesn't shift in a memo. It shifts when new behaviors feel real and visible.

DURABILITY (Presence + Sustainability)

Q1 Goal: Show up calm and provide strategic signal without being a reactive firefighter.

Month 1

- **Objective:** Audit his own presence

- **Experiment:** Record two meetings, watch them without sound, and journal the patterns

- **Measure:** Number of presence shifts identified, clarity and steadiness score

Month 3

- **Objective:** Run a mini 360

- **Experiment:** Ask three peers to describe his leadership tone now

- **Measure:** Alignment with the brand he's trying to project

No slide decks here. Just raw reflection on how leadership presence shows up when it counts.

David didn't try to do everything. He chose what mattered, kept it real, and focused on forward motion. Every experiment connected back to a goal, and every goal linked to a milestone. The whole system aimed at traction, not theater. This is how your 90-day L.E.A.D. Laboratory works. It's not theory. It's your leadership, operationalized.

Sarah's 90-Day L.E.A.D. Plan

David's a CTO. Sarah's not. She's a Senior Director of Ops, smart, strategic, and already doing half the work of someone with a VP title, minus the pay and visibility. This quarter isn't just about fixing team problems. It's about signaling that she's ready to lead at the next level.

Her twelve-month vision was sharp: She's no longer the firefighter-in-chief. Her team moves with clarity, escalates less, and solves more. Her calendar reflects her priorities, not just everybody else's chaos. She's known for systems thinking, building leadership around her, and holding the line on what matters.

That's the vision. Here's how she built her Q1 milestone and flywheel.

Q1 Milestone:

Install repeatable leadership rhythms that shift decision ownership down-stream and lift Sarah out of reactive problem-solving.

LEAN (Strategic Focus)

Goal: Align team focus with business impact.

Month 1

- **Objective:** Run a "Mission to Metrics" workshop

- **Experiment:** Map each team's work to a clear business win

- **Measure:** Team clarity score (can they articulate purpose in their own words?)

EMPOWER (Ownership Structures)

Goal: Build a stronger middle layer of decision-makers.

Month 2

- **Objective:** Clarify decision-making roles

- **Experiment:** Use the Decision Lens with each team lead

- **Measure:** Fewer escalations, more confident calls from directs

AMPLIFY (Cultural Narrative)

Goal: Reinforce a proactive team identity.

Month 3

- **Objective:** Launch a recurring ritual

- **Experiment:** "Friday Foresight," weekly share-out of smart bets and lessons

- **Measure:** Participation rate, signs of strategic thinking showing up across levels

DURABILITY (Personal Sustainability)

Goal: Protect strategic focus through visible boundaries.

Month 1

- **Objective:** Block two "CEO Hours" per week

- **Experiment:** Use those hours for reflection, planning, and signal-setting

- **Measure:** Calendar integrity, visible shift in how she shows up

Month 3

- **Objective:** Get feedback on leadership tone

- **Experiment:** Self-led 360 with peers and directs

- **Measure:** Qualitative input on how her presence is landing

That's Sara's three flywheels. They're lean, focused, and have no filler. She didn't try to fix everything. She picked the levers that would shift her role, lift her team, and build real momentum toward the next level of leadership and focused intentionally on them.

A Note Before You Start Your Own Lab

If you're reading all this and thinking, "That's a lot of work," you're right. Designing a real 90-Day L.E.A.D. Laboratory isn't something to rush through, especially the first time. This is your leadership blueprint, your operating system upgrade. It deserves thought, honesty, and focus. The goal isn't to fill boxes for the sake of it. It's to get clear on what really matters, choose the levers that will move you forward, and set up experiments that deliver momentum you can see and feel.

I built the VIP Intensive because I believe so strongly in how much this matters, and how much it has already helped leaders I work with. It's a focused, one-on-one four-hour session where we work together to design your full 90-day plan, lock in clear objectives, and shape experiments that actually fit your context, your team, and your goals.

You don't need more theory. You need a plan you'll actually use.

The Myth We're Breaking

Let's stop right here before anyone starts nodding politely and thinking, "Oh, okay, so this is just a fancy new way to plan."

No. It's not.

If you're still reading this like it's a productivity framework with better formatting, you've missed the point. This isn't a planning tool. This is a leadership operating system. One built to move when it counts, adjust in real time, and keep you learning faster than your job can bury you in chaos.

The myth we're breaking is this: **If the plan is solid, we just need to execute.**

Cute idea. If leadership was a bake sale, maybe that would work. But you and I both know how this goes. The second you launch that shiny new plan, reality drops in with fire drills, reorgs, competing priorities, and a surprise resignation just to keep things fun. A strategy that only works in a perfect world isn't a strategy. It's fiction. Thankfully, your leadership isn't defined by perfection. It's defined by how quickly you spot cracks, and how willing you are to fix them before they spread.

Every 90-day plan is a hypothesis, every experiment inside it is a bet, and every bet needs a feedback loop, or it turns into a slow-motion trainwreck. The leaders who break through aren't the ones who stick to the original blueprint no matter what. They're the ones who built the second, third, and fourth versions while everyone else was still clinging to the first. They don't waste time defending old decisions. They stay close to the signals, close to the team, and close to what's actually working. That's what separates leaders who coast through "execution" and leaders who stay dangerous.

You're not here to execute a flawless plan. You're here to build momentum by iterating in real conditions, adjusting in real time, and staying sharp while the game keeps changing.

Now let's talk about the flywheel itself, and how the weekly rhythm becomes your new engine.

The 30-Day Flywheel: Rhythm in Motion

Your 90-day L.E.A.D. Lab is only as good as the rhythm behind it. Without that, it's just a spreadsheet waiting to be ignored. The work isn't to *launch* the plan. The work is to *run* it, *watch* it, and *adjust* it, week by week, while the game is still shifting under your feet.

That's why the flywheel exists.

It's the core is your **weekly rhythm**. Act, reflect, adjust. No long-winded postmortems. No waiting until Month 3 to realize you've been measuring the wrong thing. Just a tight, deliberate loop that keeps the momentum alive and the signal sharp.

I usually don't like to say things like "here's the truth," because it begs the question, "What? Have you been lying to me?" In all my experience, I know this one truth:

Leaders with rhythm outperform leaders with "perfect plans" every time.

Not because they're smarter, but because they're in motion. They're learning. They're adjusting before the wheels fall off. Rhythm is what keeps progress real. Rhythm is what turns leadership from performance art into traction.

This is where you build three essential muscles:

- **Awareness.** What's actually happening, not what you hoped would happen.

- **Adaptation.** How to adjust without losing sight of the goal.

- **Acceleration.** When to double down because the signal is real.

To train those muscles, you need structure. Not a "check-in." A cadence. A fast, focused, relentless loop that keeps leadership honest. This is where we introduce what 4DX calls the **Cadence of Accountability**, a weekly loop that asks three simple, ruthless questions:

- **Account.** What did we say we'd do?

- **Review.** What actually happened? What signals showed up?

- **Plan.** What do we do now? Reinforce, pivot, or shut it down?

That's it. No fluff. No excuses. No dashboards with 47 metrics. Just one loop, every week. And it matters more than anything else you've built so far, because **without rhythm, even the best strategy turns to noise**. That's not theory. That's a clearly visible pattern. Week after week, leaders who stay in motion and stay in the loop don't just survive change. They start weaponizing it.

So, you're not waiting 30 days to "evaluate the flywheel." You're not waiting for a quarterly review to finally get honest. Your flywheel runs on rhythm, and that rhythm holds three nested loops:

- **Weekly loop.** Keeps your experiments alive and sharp.

- **Monthly loop.** Adjusts your 30-60-90-day objectives based on what's actually working.

- **Quarterly loop.** Builds your next 90-day L.E.A.D. Lab, as part of a larger *ascent loop*.

THE RHYTHM OF
DURABLE LEADERSHIP

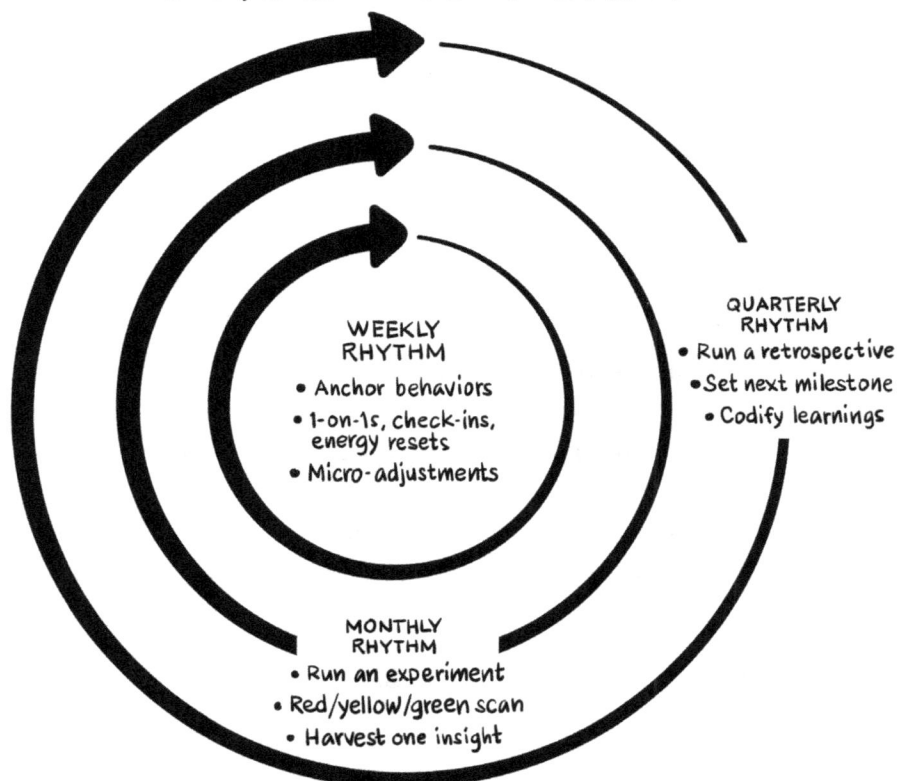

WEEKLY RHYTHM
- Anchor behaviors
- 1-on-1s, check-ins, energy resets
- Micro-adjustments

QUARTERLY RHYTHM
- Run a retrospective
- Set next milestone
- Codify learnings

MONTHLY RHYTHM
- Run an experiment
- Red/yellow/green scan
- Harvest one insight

These loops aren't "agile." They're just smart. And remember this: Not all experiments are team-based. Some are for you. We covered this back in Chapters 7 through 10: Experiments can focus on personal leadership growth, team behavior, or even org-wide shifts. Some experiments are just for your own development, like shifting how you show up in meetings or setting better boundaries. Others are meant for your team or department to run together. And some you could run either way. But regardless of scope, the rhythm is non-negotiable.

If it's your own experiment, you might track it solo, or debrief with a coach, mentor, or peer. If it's a team experiment, you might make the scoreboard visible and build a shared cadence. Either way, you need the rhythm. Personal or collective, **the cycle still applies**. Leadership development doesn't get a pass just because the experiment is "about you." You don't get to skip rhythm and call it reflection. This system works because it's built to run, to learn, and to evolve while the work is still in motion.

Leadership gains traction when rhythm replaces rigidity. When you lead inside this system, you stop guessing and start iterating with purpose. You stop managing tasks and start reading signal. You don't need clairvoyance. You need cadence.

The real killer isn't bad planning, it's the absence of rhythm. But you're not here to drift. You're here to lead in motion.

David's First Pivot: When the Plan Flexes

Month Two was supposed to be smooth sailing.

David had lined everything up. Two tech-led bets were live. Alignment sessions were done. Ownership was supposedly clear. But halfway through the month, things stalled. One of his initiative leads went quiet. Cross-functional partners started asking the same questions twice. A key decision got kicked back up to David, even though it should've been handled downstream.

It was a textbook moment where momentum falters due to friction in the system.

He could've blamed the lead, or the plan, or the org's "lack of execution discipline." He could've waited to see if it would all smooth out in a week or two. It's tempting, just give it more time and hope it fixes itself. Instead, in our next session, David came in tight-jawed and tired.

"Jim," he said, "I don't get it. We were rolling. The structure's there. Everyone nodded along. So why does it feel like I'm back in the center again?"

I asked, "David, what's the actual signal?"

He exhaled. "People are hesitating. The leads aren't owning decisions. It's starting to loop back through me."

"And what do you think that's about?"

"Honestly? I think they're unclear. They didn't push back in the meetings, but I'm realizing they may not really get what we're trying to do here."

"So, what are they executing, clarity or assumption?"

He paused. Then shook his head. "Assumption. That's on me."

That was the pivot. David pulled back from the delegation sprint and ran a new experiment: clarify the win conditions. One-on-one, no decks, no meetings, just clear, human conversations. He didn't ask if people "got it." He asked them to walk the goal back to him, in their own words.

That move reactivated the lane. Not because the plan changed, but because the leadership did.

David didn't panic. He didn't double down. He didn't defend the original design like it was sacred. He read the signal and moved. Fast enough to make a difference. Calm enough to keep his credibility intact. That's exactly what the flywheel is built for.

Not to run a perfect plan, but to keep you learning while the game is still live.

Leadership isn't about making the right decision once. It's about building the rhythm that helps you keep making the next right one, again and again.

Scoreboards vs. Dashboards (Applied)

You already know the difference: dashboards track noise, scoreboards track momentum. Dashboards explain the past; scoreboards fuel the next move. So, let's make it real. At this level, a scoreboard isn't decoration, it's direction. It shows you whether the work is working. A good scoreboard here does three things:

1. **Tracks progress toward your swimlane goals.** Each L.E.A.D. swimlane should have clear lead measures, signals that show if you're actually moving toward your Q1 objectives.

2. **Surfaces energy trends.** Is the team leaning in, or checking out? Are experiments sparking momentum, or quietly stalling?

3. **Makes micro-wins visible.** These aren't vanity metrics. They're early indicators that something is catching, spreading, or lifting belief.

That's it. If it doesn't help you focus, it doesn't belong.

Below is a sample scoreboard David used to track his Q1 lab, not to impress execs, but to guide the real work, week by week.

Scoreboard Example – David's Q1 Lab

Swimlane	Lead Measure Example	Micro-Win Example	Energy Trend
Lean	% of team who can explain initiative's "why"	A peer exec uses the strategy spine unprompted	Up/Flat/Down
Empower	# of decisions made without David's involvement	Initiative lead escalates *less* and decides *more*	Up/Flat/Down
Amplify	# of Slack/email stories shared about early wins	Another team borrows the same ritual or language	Up/Flat/Down
Durability	# of meetings David shows up with full presence	Peer feedback reflects tone shift ("you seemed calmer")	Up/Flat/Down

They're not for show. They're for action. In your weekly cadence, you'll look at them to assess whether each experiment is green, yellow, or red. In your monthly reset, they tell you where to double down or pivot. In your quarterly review, they expose the patterns that shape your next ascent.

This isn't data theater. It's **leadership traction in real time**. Most importantly, scoreboards guide **the conversation inside your flywheel rhythm**.

Coach's Commentary

Dashboards tell stories about the past. Scoreboards give you the guts to change the story now.

Staying in the Game: Weekly Check-Ins

Let's get this straight: the weekly check-in is not group therapy. It's not a status meeting. It's not your chance to hold the mic and narrate your week like it's a TED Talk. This is where your **operating system is set in motion**.

1. Account

What did I say I'd do last week? That's it. Not what you meant to do. Not what you almost did. Not a novella about your calendar. Just the actual commitment you made out loud, in front of other people.

2. Report

Where are we now, Red, Yellow, or Green?

- Green means it's on track.
- Yellow means it's progressing but with risk.
- Red means it's stalled, stuck, or sliding backward.

This is **not** your moment to explain, justify, or take us on a six-slide detour. It's signal, not story. The only rule: **No color? No credibility.** And no half-colors either. No "sort of green with a hint of yellow." No hedging. Pick one and own it.

3. Plan

What's the next step between now and our next meeting? This is where you make a clear, visible move. Do you keep going? Tweak it? Kill it and pivot to something smarter? Doesn't need to be fancy. It needs to be **real**.

Here's what it sounds like when done right:

"Last week, I said I'd run alignment sessions for Bet #2. I ran one, the other got bumped. Yellow. Next week I'm rescheduling that second one, and I'll pulse-check buy-in after both."

That's it. That's the move. Done in under a minute. No oxygen theft. No TED audition. And if you do this across your core experiments, whether individual or team-based, every single week, you'll no longer just be crossing your fingers and hoping for the best. You'll be tracking signal while you're in motion. You'll be leading.

And just so we're crystal clear: If your experiment doesn't map to the scoreboard, it doesn't belong in the lab. Bad experiment, bad measure, or bad honesty. Pick one and fix it. This isn't theater. This is traction. And leadership that can't handle a one-minute check-in probably isn't ready to own the quarter.

End-of-Flywheel Reset: The 30-Day Review

Let's get something out of the way, **this is not a postmortem**. This isn't where we spend 90 minutes diagnosing why things feel "off" and assigning labels in a Miro board no one will look at again.

This is a reset. A mid-battle course correction. A leadership tune-up.

You've just completed your first 30-day flywheel. That means the lab isn't theoretical anymore. It's live. You've got signal, real data from real experiments. Now the job is to make that signal actionable. This moment adds **another level to the cadence of accountability.** Just like your weekly rhythm, this reset follows a sharp sequence:

- **Account:** What experiments did we say we'd run?

- **Report:** Which objectives were we aiming to shift? Were they actually reached, yes or no?

Planning comes next, but **not here yet**. We'll go deeper on that in Chapter 12. Right now, your job is to **tighten the loop** without overhauling the whole damn lab. Here's how:

✅ Red/Yellow/Green Scan

For every active experiment, call the color:

- Green = Accelerate

- Yellow = Tweak or reinforce

- Red = Kill it or fix it fast

No detours. No justifications. Just the facts.

✅ Scoreboard Update

Check your lead measures. Are they moving? Are they showing up in behavior? Are they updated weekly? If not, either your scoreboard's broken, or you stopped using it.

✅ One Move Per Swimlane

Look across the four L.E.A.D. lanes:

- Accelerate one thing that's working

- Tweak or reinforce one thing that's at risk

- Drop any dead weight, no apologies

That's how momentum builds. Not from overhauling. From smart, visible moves in the right places.

You'll lock in your next flywheel moves in Chapter 12, but before we shift forward, hit reset with intent.

☑ Recommit

Now that the noise is cleared, recommit. Not with a shrug. With intent. Reset your next 30 days like it's Day 1 again. Because it is. And yes, **all experiments should wrap at this point**. If something didn't finish, that's not a default extension, it's a decision point. Either extend it *intentionally*, with a new commitment and measure, or shut it down and start smarter. Don't carry half-baked tests into the next flywheel. They'll just rot and confuse everything.

How this flywheel ends will shape what comes next.

Coach's Commentary

Momentum doesn't die from failure. It dies from neglect. Mid-course correction is not a luxury, it's oxygen. Tighten the loop.

Driving Question

Am I leading my 90-day Labatory, or am I letting it lead me?

Your Coaching Question From Jim

☞ At the one-month checkpoint, what one adjustment would make the next 60 days radically more powerful, more visible, or more strategic?

Mini Challenge: The 30-Day Flywheel Reset

✐ Download Worksheet: W11 – 30-Day Experiment Health Scan

Challenge Steps:

- Run a Red/Yellow/Green scan on each active experiment

- Update your scoreboard (no dashboard bloat allowed)

- Pick one experiment to accelerate with intention

- Pick one to adjust, support, or kill

- Write one leadership decision you're making today to shape the next 30 days

Reminder: This isn't about being perfect. This is about keeping the wheel spinning, with smarter energy each cycle.

Final Reframe: Rhythm Wins, Not the Plan

☞ If you remember nothing else from this chapter, remember this: **Rhythm is what keeps your leadership alive.**

Weekly rhythm, monthly rhythm, quarterly rhythm. That's the system. That's the edge. The plan will bleed, the scoreboard will bend, and the map you thought you could trust will punch you straight in the mouth.

Good. Because leadership isn't built during clean launches. It's built in the mess, in the mid-flight pivots, in the decisions you make when certainty's already gone.

If you're waiting for perfect clarity, perfect timing, perfect alignment? You're already behind. You don't lead by waiting for things to be stable. You lead by adapting faster than the chaos.

You want to lead like a CEO? Then be the architect who rewrites the playbook mid-game and still wins. This isn't your victory lap. This isn't your postmortem. This is your **mid-battle reload**.

In the next chapter, you'll learn how to tighten the flywheel even further. Not just surviving change, but by **weaponizing it.**

CHAPTER 12

Mid-Cycle Mastery, Adjust Without Losing Altitude

Real leaders don't cling to broken experiments.
They fix fast and move forward.

– Jim Saliba

Hope Is Not a Leadership Strategy

I didn't plan to hear a leadership train wreck over Sunday tea (I know you're asking, "A New Yorker not drinking coffee?" What can I tell you? That's me), but there it was, one of the top execs from a major company, smiling for the cameras, explaining a stalled initiative with this little gem: "We're doing this because we hope it will get us there." I put the cup down. Hard. Hope? That's your plan?

It reminded me of that line from *Grumpy Old Men*: "Hope is for suckers." And yet, there it is. In town halls, in strategy decks, in offsite recaps. Leaders betting the next 60 days on optimism instead of action. Crossing fingers instead of reading the data.

Hope is not a move. Hope doesn't fix an unsteady plan. Hope doesn't pull you out of a nosedive. Hope isn't strategy; it's denial dressed up in a blazer.

You want to be the pilot, not the passenger. Pilots don't wait until the cabin shakes to check their gauges. They scan early, they adjust in flight, they fly the damn plane even when the air gets rough.

Chapter 11 gave you your first flight plan. You launched your 90-day L.E.A.D. Lab, ran the first flywheel, and tracked momentum in real time. Now it's time to level up. This chapter introduces the monthly adjustment loop, the moment where you use real data to sharpen the next 30 days while there's still time to move the needle. Whether you've just closed your first flywheel or wrapped your second, this is where you tune the next one based on what's actually working, not what you hoped would work.

Not a reset. Not a panic. Not a brand-new plan. Just smart leadership in motion. Because leadership isn't about clinging to what you meant to do. It's about owning what the signals are telling you and adjusting while there's still time to make the next cycle smarter.

The Myth We're Breaking: "Let's Give It More Time"

There's a sentence that kills more momentum than any external threat ever could: "We just need to give it more time." Leaders say it with a straight face, as if patience alone will untangle fuzzy roles, fix a misaligned experiment, or make a team suddenly care. It's the professional version of crossing your fingers and waiting for magic.

Time does not fix bad bets. It does not sharpen blurry goals. It does not reward you for being polite with the wrong strategy. Time is neutral. Learning is what moves the needle. People love to say "fail fast," but what that really means is **listen fast**. Don't wait for perfect clarity. Don't cling to the first draft of the plan like it's sacred. "Fail fast" isn't about being reckless; it's about being responsive. Spot the risks early and adjust while you still have runway.

Stalling out rarely comes from making the wrong move. It comes from not moving fast enough when the signal says, "This isn't working." Waiting, rationalizing, hoping. That delay costs more than any single mistake. Now you don't wait for perfect clarity. You don't keep a limp experiment on life support out of loyalty to the original plan. You don't even need to be right on the first try. You just need to see what's not working and adjust while there's still altitude to work with.

Leadership isn't about defending your initial moves. It's about recognizing drift, naming it out loud, and course-correcting before the next 30 days go down the drain.

Where This Loop Lives in the System

You already know the weekly flywheel rhythm: act, reflect, adjust. That's your real-time feedback loop to keep experiments alive and aligned. It's fast, focused, and brutally honest. But it's not the only loop in play.

Every 30 days, something different kicks in. You're not just checking on tasks anymore. You're stepping back to ask: Are these experiments actually moving the objectives we set? Are those objectives still the right ones? And if not, what are we doing about it?

This is your monthly loop. It's not about evaluation. It's about evolution. It's the moment to catch drift before it becomes a tailspin, to sharpen goals while the game is still live, and to make the next flywheel sharper than the last.

Then comes the quarterly loop. That's where we zoom all the way out. You'll reflect across the full 90-day L.E.A.D. Lab, run a retro, and redesign the next ascent cycle with fresh data. That loop is about integrating what you've learned and designing what's next.

Here's the bonus that so many leaders miss: When you run your monthly loop well, when you adjust smartly and decisively, you don't just improve the next flywheel. You start evolving the milestone itself. Sometimes, you see so clearly what's working that you shift the next milestone forward. Sometimes, the progress is strong enough that you stretch the 12-month vision. You're not abandoning strategy. You're advancing it.

This isn't just a calendar reminder. It's a leadership muscle. The monthly loop is what separates hopeful plans from real momentum.

The 30-Day Adjustment Framework

You've just completed your first 30-day flywheel. Your experiments have run their course; some landed, some faltered, some flatlined. Now it's time to do what strong leaders actually do: learn from the data and adjust forward.

Before we dive into how to adjust, let's anchor back to how each experiment was built. In Chapter 7, we defined a real leadership experiment as having six parts:

- A **question or challenge** you're trying to understand or fix

- A **hypothesis** you're testing

- An **experiment**, a specific, action to test that hypothesis

- A **timeframe**, because without one, these things drag on forever

- A **success measure**, a visible signal that tells you if it's working

- A **reflection**, where you stop, look back , and actually learn

You used these to power your first flywheel. In Chapter 11, you tracked them with rhythm using the cadence of accountability:

- **Account.** What did we say we'd do?

- **Report.** What actually happened?

- **Plan.** What's next, based on what we now know?

You've already covered account and report. Now we shift to the third part: plan. And not in the "what are my next five tasks" sense. This is the leadership-level plan: Do we adjust the objectives? Refine our swimlane goals? Push out a milestone? Pull something forward?

You've now got real data, results, signals, and patterns. You don't have to guess anymore. You've seen what moved and what stalled. You've seen where energy lives and where friction keeps showing up. This is where you use that insight to update, not restart, your direction.

This next 30-day cycle isn't a rerun, but it's not a rewrite either. You're still running the plan you set. What changes now is how you move inside it: sharper focus, tighter feedback, better signal. You're adjusting your execution, not your strategy. Here's how to do it.

Step 1: Red, Yellow, Green Every Experiment

Start here. Not with storytelling, not with optimism, with the signal. And get brutally honest about it. This isn't just a post-mortem. It's a systems check.

Every experiment was designed to drive an objective, every objective was chosen to move a 90-day swimlane goal, and each goal was mapped to your quarterly milestone. That's the chain. Now it's time to ask: Is the chain holding?

This isn't just a "what went well" retro. It's a systems check across all four swimlanes. Ask yourself:

- Did each experiment actually hit its designed objective?

- Did that objective create real movement toward the swimlane goal?

- Does that goal still represent the right signal in this lane?

- Are we still tracking toward the quarterly milestone, or are we drifting?

Because sometimes the experiment "works" but moves nothing that matters. Sometimes the objective was solid, but the execution flopped. And sometimes, the goal itself is off, and it's time to aim sharper before the next flywheel spins. That's why we run the signal scan:

Green. We hit the objective, and it's clearly moving the goal forward.
> → Lock it in. Expand scope. Build off the signal.
> Name the win so others can see and build on it.

Yellow. We made partial progress. Maybe the objective was fuzzy, the experiment landed soft, or it moved, but not enough.
> → Adjust the angle. Add structure. Add support.
> Or create a follow-up experiment to finish the job.

Red. We missed the objective. Or hit it, but it didn't matter. Or it actively made things harder.
> → Kill it clean. Or reframe it. Or step back and ask:
> Do we need to rethink the goal this was meant to serve?

Here's the heart of it:

The question isn't "Did it go well?"

The question is: "Did it move the system?"

If the answer is no, then it's time to shift. Not next month. Not when you "have more data." Now. This is your first reset moment, and it's the one that keeps the next 30 days from becoming a fancier version of the last 30 days. This is where you start weaponizing the system.

Back in Chapter 11, we said the goal wasn't to survive the flywheel, it was to sharpen it. Right here, right now, is how that happens. Surgical adjustments aren't signs of failure. They're proof you're paying attention. Dropping a bad experiment isn't quitting. It's leadership with teeth. It's the difference between running the playbook and rewriting it mid-game because you're smart enough to see the pivot and fast enough to make it count.

You're still inside your 90-day Laboratory, but you're not locked in. This monthly checkpoint is where the best leaders create separation by injecting smarter experiments, sharpening goals, and realigning flight paths before drift turns into failure. Because that's what your leadership looks like. Not running blindly through all 90 days, but stopping the drift, making the call, and turning your plan into a weapon.

Coach's Commentary: Adjustment ≠ Failure

Changing course doesn't mean you failed. Waiting too long to change? That's the real failure.

Step 2: Recalibrate the Scoreboard

Let's talk signal, not noise. You've already run the experiment. You've scanned the results. Now ask yourself: Is the scoreboard helping us *lead*, or just observe? This isn't about color-coded clutter or a dashboard that makes your slide deck look smart. A scoreboard has one job: to make signal visible so decisions get sharper, faster. And not all metrics are created equal. Some just take up space. Some feel nice but mean nothing. Some distract more than they direct. So, here's your scoreboard gut check:

- Are we tracking **lead measures**, the stuff that drives behavior and creates momentum?

- Is the scoreboard helping us see progress *early*, before it's too late to adjust?

- Can a human glance at this and know what matters this week?

- Is it emotionally relevant, or just data wallpaper?

Scoreboard Filter Checklist

Use this to decide what stays — and what gets cut.

KEEP a scoreboard metric if it...

☑ Drives real behavior (people act because of it)

☑ Shows early signal, not just outcomes

☑ Is reviewed regularly in your weekly rhythm

☑ Sparks decisions or questions

☑ Makes the flywheel sharper, not noisier

KILL a scoreboard metric if it...

☑ Sits untouched for a week or more

☑ Only looks good on a slide deck

☑ Tracks activity without showing traction

☑ Gets mentioned but never changes anything

☑ Feels like a leftover from the last strategy cycle

If your scoreboard doesn't help your team (or yourself) act, it's not a scoreboard. It's an artifact. A decoration. A meeting prop. This is the moment to tune it. Tighten it. Strip out the bloat. Highlight the few things that tell you whether your flywheel is flying or flaming out. This isn't about "measuring everything." It's about **clarifying what matters most**, so your next set of moves aren't based on vibes or opinions, they're based on visible, shared signal.

Scoreboards don't just reflect progress. They *shape* it. And when you get them right, they do half the alignment work for you.

Coach's Commentary: If It Doesn't Provoke, It's Wallpaper

A scoreboard should spark decisions, not decorate meetings. If it's not changing behavior, fix it or ditch it.

Step 3: Re-anchor One Swimlane

Let's clear this up: You might tweak a few things across the board. That's fine. But you don't need to (and shouldn't) go into overhaul mode across all four swimlanes. What you **do** need is to choose one lane to re-anchor with real focus and force.

The goal here is clarity, not cleanup. Pick the swimlane that, if sharpened, would have the biggest impact on your momentum toward the milestone. That's the one that gets the deep energy. Ask yourself:

- Which lane is closest to unlocking the milestone?

- Where's the most drift, or the biggest opportunity?

- What's the one experiment in that lane that could shift the game?

Re-anchor that lane. Get crisp. Choose one clear move:

- Double down on what's working.

- Replace what's stalling.

- Refine the goal if it no longer fits what the system actually needs.

And yes, you can do light tuning in the other lanes. But don't spread your leadership energy like peanut butter. You're not here to gently improve everything. You're here to move the whole thing forward, and that starts with going all-in where it counts most.

Leadership isn't about balancing effort. It's about choosing impact.

Step 4: Reset the Commitment Loop

This is the moment you're tempted to skip. You assume everyone's already "aligned," or you cross your fingers and hope the system fixes itself. It won't. And neither will you, if you pretend the original plan doesn't need edits.

You just completed a full flywheel. You've scanned your experiments, adjusted the scoreboard, and re-anchored your focus. Now you reset, not because everything broke, but because you're not standing still. This is the point where strong leaders recommit, not to the original plan, but to the sharper, smarter version of it. This is not Version 2.0. That's the move people make when they're trying to disguise a failure as a fresh start. This is Version 1.2.

That means the system worked well enough to teach you something. Now you're reinforcing what matters, dropping what doesn't, and stepping into the next 30 days with a tighter focus and stronger signal. So say it. With your team, with your coach, or just with yourself. Say:

- "Here's what we're doubling down on."

- "Here's what we're adjusting."

- "Here's what we're no longer pretending is fine."

This is how momentum gets built: through conscious recommitment, not default behavior. If you don't say what's changing, don't be surprised when nothing does.

Strong leaders don't just adjust the plan. They adjust the energy behind it.

Coach's Commentary: Don't Fake Alignment

Recommitting without recalibrating is just noise. If nothing real shifted, don't pretend it did.

Story: How Michael Turned the Corner (Just in Time)

Michael had kicked off his first L.E.A.D. Laboratory with real energy. Clear vision, sharp experiments, and full buy-in from his team. His first 30-day flywheel was in motion, and on paper, things looked solid. But when we got into our session, something was off.

He opened with, "Jim, I think we just need to give it more time."

"Time for what?" I asked.

He shrugged. "I mean... the experiments. Some of them are close. A few haven't really landed yet."

That was the red flag.

"Michael," I said, "are you still running the experiments you launched 30 days ago?"

"Well, yeah. Sort of. We've been tweaking them a little. Some of the results haven't fully come in yet."

I paused. "What happened to closing the first flywheel?"

He blinked. "We didn't. I guess we're still in it."

That was exactly the problem.

Michael wasn't moving into the second flywheel. He was lingering. Waiting. Stretching out the first batch of experiments past their shelf life.

Which meant no real reset, no recommitment, no clarity about what to stop, start, or shift.

"What would happen," I asked, "if instead of hoping these play out, you treated them like data?"

"What do you mean?"

"Close the loop. Run the R-Y-G scan. Not to evaluate effort, but to make decisions. Which experiments ended strong? Which fizzled? Which never even launched right?"

He scanned his board. Lean and Amplify were showing movement, Green. Empower was Yellow, barely engaging his directors. Durability had a Red sitting like deadweight.

"I've honestly been ignoring it," he admitted. "I've been pulled in other directions."

"So," I asked, "which swimlane gets the reset?"

Michael paused. "Empower. That one matters most to our milestone. If I don't get shared ownership by Day 60, we stall."

"Exactly," I said. "So, re-anchor it. Sharpen the objective, adjust the experiment, and kill the stuff you're dragging along just because you don't want to admit it's over."

He nodded. "Durability just needs a light touch, enough to help people experience me differently, not to make me a whole new leader like I tried to do at first. That'll support the Empower lane better. I'll redesign Empower. I'll build on the Lean lane momentum, we've got a new rhythm that's catching on fast."

And then he said the line that mattered:

"I thought I was in the middle of my first flywheel. I wasn't. I just hadn't ended it."

There it was.

Michael didn't need a new strategy. He needed to end the first flywheel, make the hard calls, and move forward with clarity. Once he did, momentum returned, not because he tried harder, but because he *led the transition.*

How Adjustments Cascade

This isn't just about fixing what broke. It's about keeping the whole system aligned.

Every adjustment you make now affects the next 30 days, and the 30 after that. That's why this isn't an isolated checkpoint. It's a hinge. So, ask yourself:

- Does this experiment carry over into the next flywheel, or does it close clean?

- Did we stretch an objective that needs a second run with tighter focus?

- Does one swimlane need to rise in priority, now that another has stabilized?

- Do we need to recast the milestone, or shift the 12-month vision altogether?

None of that means you failed. It means you're paying attention.

The best leaders don't wait for quarterly reviews to make strategic shifts. They make them now, clean, conscious, and well-timed. That's what rhythm is for. It keeps the chain tight:

Experiment → Objective → Goal → Milestone → Vision

If one link drifts, the rest do too, but if you adjust in real time, you don't just correct, you accelerate. So, close your flywheel with intent. Know what's coming with you, what's getting left behind, and what needs a sharper aim next.

Driving Question

🔹 Are you closing your 30-day flywheel with clarity, or just letting it trail off and call it progress?

Your Coaching Question From Jim

🔹 If a friend came to you and described exactly what you're living through, the same stuckness, the same signals, what bold decision would they make that would make you jealous? Now ask yourself: What's stopping me from making that move first?

Mini Challenge: 30-Day Adjustment

This is your leadership reset: fast, focused, and frictionless.

✍ Download Worksheet: W12 – Mid-Cycle Experiment Reset

Challenge Steps:

1. **Run the scan.** Call it clean. No hedging, no spin. Review every experiment, mark it green, yellow, or red, and then close the loop. Done is done.

2. **Adjust the objectives.** Don't recycle experiments. Decide which objectives still matter, then design fresh experiments to hit them. Kill what's not pulling its weight. You may need to make room. The next flywheel might need sharper focus, not just more stuff. This is where you reset expectations with yourself, your team, and your stakeholders. That's the power of the system; you're not stuck waiting. You can make smart adjustments early and communicate them before momentum slips.

3. **Reset the scoreboard.** Strip it down. Keep only the lead measures that drive behavior. If it doesn't help you act, it doesn't belong.

4. **Say your recommitment out loud.** Say it to your team, your coach, or your own reflection. Say: "Here's what I'm doubling down on. Here's what I'm shifting."

This is how real leaders lead the loop, instead of just riding it.

Final Reframe: Mid-Course Correction Is the Leadership Superpower

If you remember nothing else from this chapter, remember this:

Smart leaders don't wait to find out if the plan is broken. They check. They adjust. They move.

You don't need more patience. You need more rhythm. This isn't about giving every idea a longer runway. It's about deciding, based on real signal, what's worth accelerating, what needs a sharper edge, and what's holding you back.

The 30-day flywheel isn't a box to check. It's the pressure test. And this reset? It's where leadership actually happens. The weak leader waits for a quarterly review and hopes it all comes together. The strong one makes sharper moves right now, with the system still in motion.

You want to lead like a CEO? Then act like it. Make the adjustment, recommit with force, and lead the next flywheel like you mean it. Because in Chapter 13, we zoom out. You'll step back, run your first full 90-day retrospective, extract what actually worked, and build your next L.E.A.D. Lab with stronger insight, sharper experiments, and real momentum.

This is where leadership gets compounding.

CHAPTER 13

Retrospect and Celebrate, The 90-Day Leadership Harvest

If you don't stop to extract the learning,
your team will just repeat the last 90 days on a loop.

– Jim Saliba

The past 90 days weren't just about running experiments. They were about climbing. Step 6 of the Six-Step Leadership Challenge is where that ascent starts paying off. It's where leadership growth becomes visible and durable.

Whether you've been running this lab as a solo leader or guiding an entire team, the goal is the same. You're not here to look back and high-five survival. You're here to **harvest every lesson, every signal, every insight** the last 90 days revealed. This is vital, because elevation in leadership isn't accidental. It's engineered through reflection, refinement, and conscious evolution.

You're not repeating the same quarter. You're stacking elevation.

A friend and former boss, Rob, used to say, "One data point is a dot. Two is a line. Three is a trend." You've just run three full flywheels. That's not noise, it's a pattern, and now it's time to mine those patterns for signal, sharpen your system, and level up with precision. This is your growth engine, not a checklist or a recap. Each loop is a deliberate climb powered by three essential moves:

1. **Harvest the Lessons.** Extract the signals and study the friction. Name what moved and why.

2. **Lock the System Shifts.** Codify the upgrades, cement the trust, and reinforce the rhythms that worked.

3. **Design the Next Ascent.** Make sharper bets. Build smarter experiments. Lead with what you've earned.

The 90-DAY Ascent Loop

The Engine of Sustainable Leadership Growth

Lock the System Shifts

Design the Next Ascent

30-DAY Flywheels

Harvest the Lessons

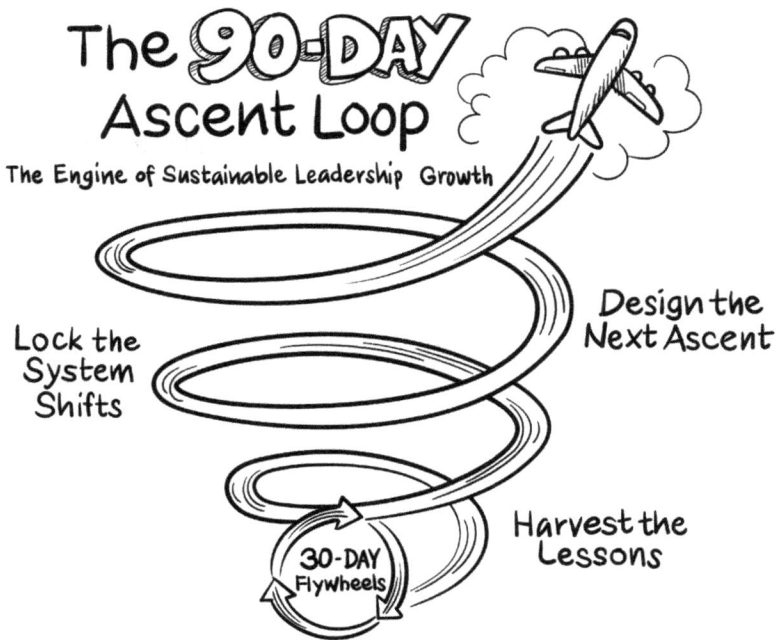

This isn't just a reflection tool. **It's your launchpad, again and again.**

The 90-Day Ascent Loop isn't about trying things and hoping they work. It's about tightening the system with each cycle, by deliberately answering three questions:

- What worked?

- What wobbled?

- What needs to move faster or sharper next time?

Done well, this process lifts everything: your leadership presence, your execution systems, your cultural impact, and your personal momentum. This chapter is about extracting the full value of the cycle you just completed, so the next 90 days don't start from zero. They start from **strength.**

You're not here to survive leadership cycles. You're here to ascend, one deliberate loop at a time. **This is Step 6 of the Six-Step Leadership Challenge.**

Whether you've been running this cycle with a full team or flying solo, the Ascent Loop applies. This is your system for pulling meaning from the mess, no matter how big or small your lab. In the earlier steps, you built visibility, empowered ownership, shaped culture, and strengthened your presence. But Step 6 is different. Step 6 is not about any single experiment or any isolated win. It is about stacking all of it, your systems, your habits, your cultural shifts, into a 90-Day Ascent Loop.

The 90-Day Ascent Loop is what separates leaders who stay busy from leaders who build momentum.

It is called an ascent for a reason. Every time you complete this loop with discipline and reflection, you're not simply circling; you're climbing. You are lifting yourself, your team, and your organization to higher levels of execution, trust, and strategic impact.

You don't get better just because time passed. You get better because you harvested the hell out of what time taught you. And that harvest starts now. You've just completed three 30-day flywheels, each one a cycle of learning, challenge, and growth. This isn't a recap of random activity. This is the moment where the patterns emerge.

Too many leaders skip this step. They slam the door on the last cycle, high-five survival, slap a few dashboards together, and charge into the next one, barely breathing, never pausing long enough to ask what actually worked, what dragged them sideways, or what deserves to be carried forward, and then they wonder why the same patterns keep kicking them in the teeth.

This work isn't about surviving quarters. It's about harvesting them. You didn't survive 90 days of experiments, pivots, and pressure just to skip the payday. You earned insights. You earned leverage. You earned the right to get smarter. But you only collect all these things you've earned if you actually stop and harvest them. Right now, you're sitting on three kinds of gold.

- **Proof**: What moves worked, undeniably, visibly, measurably.

- **Patterns**: What dynamics, behaviors, and systems either accelerated or sabotaged your leadership.

- **Power Moves**: What bold next experiments could push you even farther, if you have the guts to name them.

Skip that harvest, and you don't just risk a flat next loop. You invite a slide backward. The graveyard is full of people who learned nothing from their own hard-earned bruises, and you don't want to join them.

So let's get to work.

The Myth We're Breaking: "We already know what happened. Why waste time looking back?"

That's not reflection. That's just denial with a calendar invite. Most teams treat retrospectives like dentist appointments: They know they should do them, but they delay them until something hurts, and then they show up half-engaged, hoping to get out without too much pain. And nothing changes.

Step 6 is different. It's not a recap, it's a harvest. Not to admire the quarter, but to dissect it. What worked? What stalled? What surprised you? Your original plan had blind spots. Some experiments flopped, some wins came from moves you didn't expect, and some friction revealed leverage you didn't know you had.

The leaders who grow fast aren't the ones who defend their plans. They're the ones who interrogate them, steal lessons from friction, and build the next loop with eyes wide open.

The 90-Day Retrospective Harvest Framework

You're not here to check a box. You're here to harvest the work you've earned. Over the last 90 days, you ran experiments, responded in the moment, and tightened your leadership flywheel. Now it's time to pull the real value out of the cycle before momentum fades and memory softens.

This is not a post-mortem. It's not an excuse to admire how busy you were. This is structured leadership reflection that forces you to see what actually moved, what stalled, and what needs to be built next. It's the bridge between surviving the cycle and stacking it into strategic ascent.

Here's the framework:

1. **Run the 90-Day Experiment Review.** Revisit every experiment with the power of hindsight. No spin. No justifications. Just signals. Look at each experiment in context: Did it hit its objective? Did that objective move the goal? Did the goal meaningfully push the milestone forward, or was the ladder misaligned? This is where you assess the integrity of the full chain.

2. **Spot Swimlane Trends.** Zoom out. Don't just tally wins and losses, look for patterns across the four L.E.A.D. lanes. Where did momentum build and spread? Where did friction stall progress? Did one lane lift or drag the others? Trends at this level show you not just what worked, but *how* your system behaves under real conditions.

3. **Draft Your Forward Moves List.** Translate patterns into smart, next-cycle action. You're not guessing. You're designing forward moves drawn from real insight. Whether you're adjusting milestones, refining goals, or sharpening objectives, this is where you shape your next 90-day L.E.A.D. Lab using lived experience, not abstract theory.

4. **Capture the Cultural Signals.** Culture isn't a vibe. It's the undercurrent and terrain, and it shifted. Which rituals stuck? What language spread? Where did trust build or break? What got normalized or quietly rejected? These cultural signals are the clearest predictors of whether future moves will stick or stall. If you don't see them, you'll miss the next inflection point.

5. **Celebrate and Codify the Wins.** Momentum doesn't carry itself forward. You have to lock it in. Name the wins out loud. Document what worked. Codify the shifts into your systems, rituals, or onboarding. If you don't cement the gains, drift will erase them.

This harvest isn't optional. It's the line between chasing progress and compounding it. Skip it, and you're just running in circles. Nail it, and you turn every cycle into a launchpad.

Coach's Commentary

Leaders who harvest well don't just evolve faster. They outlast everyone who thought momentum alone would save them.

Why Most Retrospectives Suck (and How Yours Won't)

Retrospectives don't fail because people don't care. They fail because the structure is wrong, and the mindset is lazy. Too often, retrospectives become venting sessions. Everyone shows up late, rehashes old frustrations, points fingers at "them" (never themselves), promises to "communicate better next time," and quietly waits for the meeting to end. But nothing changes. The next time around drags the same broken habits forward, only now with more resentment baked in.

That's not a retrospective. That's a blame ritual disguised as progress. A meaningful retrospective asks better questions. It doesn't ask, "What went wrong?" It asks, "What friction revealed a deeper truth we needed to see?" It doesn't ask, "Who dropped the ball?" It asks, "Where did our system allow the ball to drop without a catch?"

The goal isn't to relive the crash. The goal is to strip the crash for parts, rebuild smarter, and fly better next time.

Coach's Commentary

You don't lead by reliving the crash. You lead by stealing the engine parts, and building something stronger that flies farther.

Story: Tonya's Retrospective Reset

Tonya Brooks, the acting COO we've followed throughout this book, had just wrapped a high-stakes 90-day push across her operations and product teams. The goals were bold, the experiments well-designed. But the outcomes? They were mixed. A couple clear wins, some confusing friction, and a few flat-out misses.

Wanting to regroup, Tonya called a retrospective. The leadership team showed up. Ten minutes in, it went sideways.

Product blamed ops for delayed handoffs. Ops pointed at vague requirements. Marketing claimed they were out of the loop. The meeting devolved into polite jabs, long explanations, and quiet resentment. When it ended, nothing had shifted, and Tonya was frustrated, not with her team, but with herself.

"This wasn't a retrospective," she said. "It was a blame festival with nicer snacks."

I didn't let that line slide. "Let's stop admiring what went wrong," I told her. "What's the one friction point that actually taught you something you can use?"

That cracked it open.

We tore up the usual script and rebuilt her retrospective around five essential questions:

- Which experiments clearly moved the needle, and why?

- Where did friction teach us something important?

- What didn't we plan for that surprised us?

- Which cultural dynamics helped, or hurt?

- What should we codify, kill, or reframe moving forward?

The next time she ran it, the tone changed fast. Her team wasn't just more honest, they were more strategic. They didn't dwell on who dropped the ball. They talked about redesigning the game.

That's the shift. Real retrospectives don't soothe feelings. They surface leverage. That clarity Tonya gained? That's the gold. And now it's your turn to mine it.

Coach's Commentary

A weak retrospective protects egos. A strong one protects progress.

Mining the Gold Beneath the Swimlanes

You've already been asking, "What did I learn?" at the end of each flywheel, but now it's time to zoom out and ask a sharper question: "What does the system want to teach me across all three?"

Remember when you built your 90-Day L.E.A.D. Laboratory grid? You didn't just fill out boxes. You mapped a real system. Across the top: 30, 60, and 90 days. Down the side: goals for each of the four swimlanes, Lean, Empower, Amplify, and Durability. And at the end of each row, one deceptively simple column: What did we learn?

That column wasn't an afterthought. It was the point. Because this isn't just about looking at one experiment or even one flywheel. It's about stepping back to see what your experiments, flywheels and swimlanes taught you across the whole system.

This isn't about what happened in a single experiment. It's about mining the full arc of your ascent for three kinds of gold:

- **Proof.** The sharp, undeniable signals that something you did worked. This is your confidence fuel.

- **Patterns.** The repeated behaviors, systems, frictions, or lifts that shaped your results. Spot the patterns, and you stop guessing.

- **Power Moves.** The smart, strategic experiments the last 90 days are begging you to try next. You're not starting from scratch. You're building smarter.

This isn't a recap. It's an excavation, and if you do it right, you don't enter your next cycle with vague ideas; you enter with leverage.

Retrospective Excavation Map

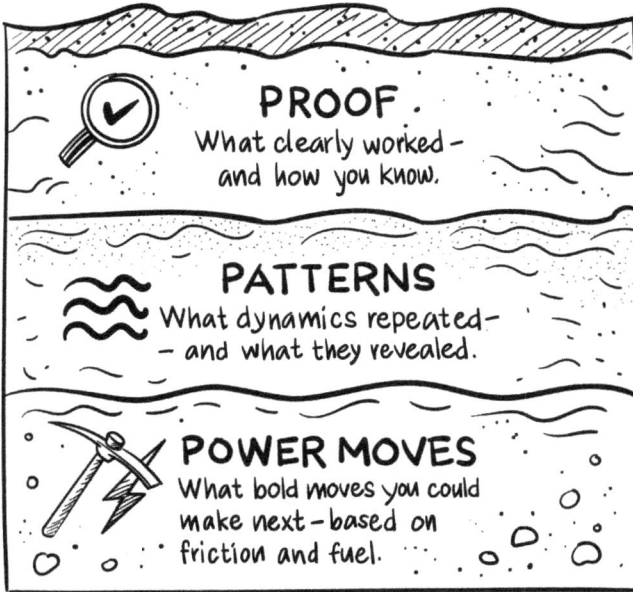

PROOF
What clearly worked —
and how you know.

PATTERNS
What dynamics repeated —
— and what they revealed.

POWER MOVES
What bold moves you could
make next — based on
friction and fuel.

How to Run a 90-Day Harvest That Actually Builds You Stronger

This isn't a postmortem. It's not a confession booth. And it's definitely not a therapy session for rehashing what went wrong. This is the turning point in your Ascent Loop, a chance to pause, reflect, and engineer your upcoming 90 days with more clarity, power, and precision.

Here's how to run a retrospective that actually sharpens your impact:

Step 1: Red / Yellow / Green the Cycle

Start by scanning your experiments. Not just where they ended up, but how they moved over time. What actually gained traction? What struggled or stalled? What burned time and energy without a return? Mark them with simple signals: green for momentum and results, yellow for friction or drift, red for missed bets or broken execution. You're not grading people. You're grading systems, choices, and team dynamics.

Step 2: Mine for Repeatable Wins

For every green or yellow zone, dig deeper. What specifically made that outcome possible? Was it the way the experiment was framed? The communication cadence? The leadership presence behind it? Identify what worked and figure out what should now become part of your operating system. Durable professionals don't just notice wins. They systematize them.

Step 3: Spot the Objectives Hiding in the Friction

Look closely at your red and yellow zones. What were they really trying to tell you? What signals point to objectives that deserve another look, clearer focus, sharper design, or different energy next time? You're not designing the next cycle yet, but you are uncovering what it *wants* to be.

Step 4: Reset Your Narrative

You're not the same person you were 90 days ago, so don't carry the same story forward. Ask yourself: What part of your leadership sharpened? What part needs to get louder, or quieter? How do you want your presence and impact to feel in the new cycle? Don't let others define your brand by accident. Redefine it with intention.

Step 5: Sample Moves That Match Your Momentum

Every lesson you've harvested points to a next step. Now is the time to turn those lessons into action. Pick one or two experiments that will build on what's working or fix what's still broken. Make them visible. Make them real. Make them run.

> ### Coach's Commentary
>
> Bad retrospectives admire the fire. Good retrospectives steal the sparks and light the fuse that fuels your ascent.

Driving Question

Are you willing to learn from reality, or are you just looking for permission to keep doing what's easy?

Your Coaching Question From Jim

Where did you feel the most resistance? Where did you feel the most lift? Design your next experiment where the real energy, and the real lesson is.

Mini Challenge: The 90-Day Ascent Loop

Download Worksheet: W13 – 90-Day Retrospective

This challenge is about converting insight into momentum.

- **Scan your original efforts: red, yellow, green.** Be honest. Celebrate what worked. Learn from what hit friction. Let go of what didn't move the needle.

- **Draft two sharp trials** you might run next, based on what the last 90 days actually taught you. Make them sharp, small, and strategic.

- **Name one cultural insight from this Ascent Loop.** What silent rule, story, or behavior pattern shaped the past 90 days, and what do you want to shift going forward?

- **Commit to one personal upgrade.** What small leadership habit will you change in the next cycle that could drive 10x more clarity, impact, or energy?

This isn't a wrap-up. This is a relaunch, wiser, sharper, and ready to build higher.

Final Reframe: The Leaders Who Win Aren't the Ones Who Guess Right

If you remember nothing else from this chapter, remember this:

The leaders who win aren't the ones who guess right the first time. They're the ones who learn faster, adjust sharper, and evolve stronger than everyone else.

They don't waste 90 days defending old moves. They run the experiments. They name the lessons. They reengineer the system, and themselves. You want to lead like a CEO? Then act like someone who doesn't just survive the game. You shape what comes after.

In Chapter 14, you'll take what you just surfaced and forge it into your next ascent loop. But don't rush. You earned this pause. Insight is only power when you pause long enough to hear it. And you just did.

CHAPTER 14

Close the Loop, Build the Next Ascent

Growth doesn't come from finishing.
It comes from looping back stronger.

– Jim Saliba

You didn't climb this far to coast. This isn't an ending. It's your ignition point. The past 90 days weren't a one-time push. They were the beginning of something bigger: a system, a flywheel, a way to climb higher with every turn. But momentum doesn't sustain itself. Real Progress doesn't scale by accident. If you don't close the loop with intention, the gains you fought for will erode, and the noise of whatever's next will bury the lessons you earned.

This is the pivot point that tests whether you'll choose to lead or just manage.

This chapter is the second half of Step 6 in the Six-Step Leadership Challenge. In Chapter 13, you harvested the signals. Now, in Chapter 14, you're going to lock in what worked, codify what matters, and prime your next ascent.

You don't grow by rushing into the next plan. You grow by stabilizing the system you just built and climbing from there.

Coach's Commentary

Most leaders treat the end of a cycle like a cooldown. Best leaders treat it like a countdown. The next level isn't a reward; it's a relaunch. Build it like you mean it

"The best move is to just ride the momentum."

It's tempting. The team feels good. Energy's up. The temptation is to keep going, no pause, no look back, no reset. But momentum without reflection isn't leadership. It's drift.

When leaders skip this moment, they miss the cracks forming under their feet. They miss the early burnout. They miss the hidden frictions that will sabotage the next cycle before it even starts. Intentional builders, on the other hand, don't just ride momentum. They stabilize, celebrate, and study it. Most importantly, they reinforce what made it possible so they can repeat it on purpose.

This chapter isn't about slowing down. It's about designing the next 90-day L.E.A.D. Laboratory. That means setting a bold new milestone, shaping fresh goals across your swimlanes, and launching stronger experiments from what you've just harvested. Drift feels easy in the moment, but it's what takes leaders off course long before they notice.

THE ASCENT ROCKET MULTPLIERS

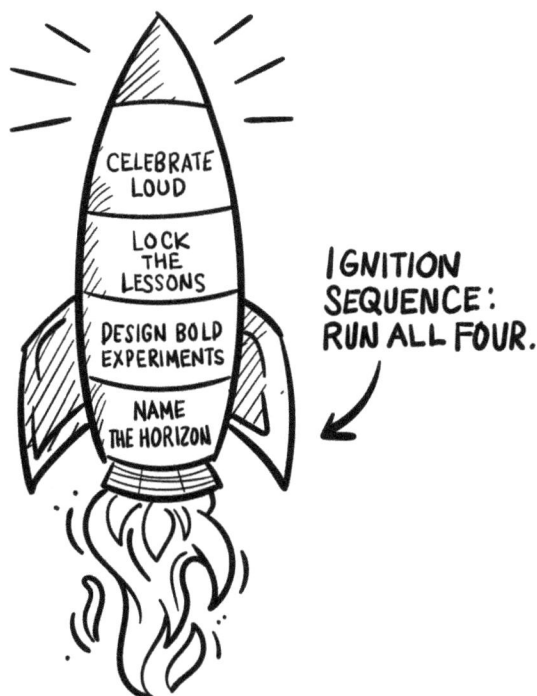

CELEBRATE LOUD

LOCK THE LESSONS

DESIGN BOLD EXPERIMENTS

NAME THE HORIZON

IGNITION SEQUENCE: RUN ALL FOUR.

Let's break this down. You're not just checking boxes. You're stacking force multipliers. Each move below builds on the others. Alone, they help. Together, they launch. Here's how leaders who mean business prime their next ascent:

Multiplier One: Celebrate Loud

Not quietly. Not later. Now. Name the system wins, the cultural shifts, the moments where your leadership showed up sharper. If you don't cement the win, your brain will only remember the struggle. **Celebration isn't fluff. It's fuel.**

Multiplier Two: Lock the Lessons

Before the noise floods back in, capture what changed. Which behaviors sharpened? What systems leveled up? What story about your leadership needs to become the new baseline? Codify it. Repeat it. **If you don't lock the lesson, you'll lose the leverage.**

Multiplier Three: Design Bold Experiments

Safe bets won't build the future. Use what you learned to shape sharper moves. Where's the real risk worth taking? What experiment will stretch you, not just sustain you?

Multiplier Four: Name the Horizon

Clarity creates energy. Say the next milestone out loud. Not a slogan, not a vague hope. A pointed direction your team can aim at. **If you don't name it, no one can commit to it.**

Now step back.

You've got four strategic multipliers, Celebrate, Lock, Design, Name. Run them together, and they don't just create alignment. **They generate ignition.** That's how you **prime the next ascent.** Because momentum isn't magic. It's engineered. You've built the flywheel. You've run the loop. Now build what's next, with purpose, with power, and with proof.

Story: How Sarah Turned Her First Ascent Loop into a Launchpad

Sarah Reynolds didn't treat her first 90-Day Ascent Loop like a checkbox. She treated it like a launchpad. Was it perfect? Not even close. Some actions wobbled. A few ideas fell flat. But Sarah didn't drift. She stayed engaged. She ran experiments across Lean, Empower, Amplify, and Durability. She adjusted at 30 days, tuned again at 60, and kept learning even when the outcomes weren't clear.

By Day 90, Sarah didn't coast to the end. She landed clean and stronger. She ran a Red/Yellow/Green scan across her full ascent loop. I asked her, "What's the one thing you built this cycle that you never want to lead without again?"

She thought for a second. "Trust," she said. "I used to think I had to push for results. But once we had clarity and rhythm, they started pulling harder than I ever could've pushed."

She named three new leadership systems she had quietly built. She spotted two blind spots that hadn't been visible on Day One. And instead of rushing forward, she paused and celebrated her team's wins, loudly and visibly.

Sarah didn't treat her first Ascent Loop like an ending. She treated it like ignition. By the time her next 90 days started, her team wasn't just ready. They were pulling harder, moving sharper, and climbing faster.

She didn't just finish the loop. She built the runway for the next one.

Step 1: Celebrate Loud, Cement the Wins Before They Fade

Celebration is the step people skip most. They tell themselves:

- "I'll celebrate when it's bigger."

- "I'll celebrate when it's perfect."

- "I'll celebrate when I have time."

Translation: I'll celebrate never.

And here's the real cost: If you don't cement your wins, your brain, and your team's, defaults to only remembering the friction, the failures, and the parts that hurt. Without celebration, the Ascent Loop feels like a slog instead of a climb. Then next cycle, when the work gets tough again (because it always does), people will quit emotionally before they even start, because they never truly felt the last victory.

Wins aren't extra. Wins are fuel.

Celebration isn't self-congratulation. It's how you anchor progress into your leadership culture. I have seen so many leaders skip this part and wonder why nothing sticks. Don't be that leader.

- **Celebrate the System Wins.** Not just the outcomes, but also what you've learned. Name the better systems you built: clarity, rhythm, trust, ownership.

- **Celebrate the Moves You Made Sharper.** What leadership moves did you sharpen? Where did you lead with more courage, clarity, or consistency?

- **Celebrate the Cultural Wins.** What invisible rules shifted because of how you showed up? What emotional norms got rewritten?

- **Celebrate the Ascent Itself.** You didn't coast. You didn't default. You climbed, even when it got messy.

You're not just congratulating effort. You're reinforcing evolution and giving your next ascent the emotional oxygen it needs to climb higher.

Step 2: Lock the Lessons, Before Life Steamrolls Them

The world doesn't care that you just ran a 90-Day Ascent Loop. It's waiting to flood you with new fires, new noise, and new distractions. If you don't capture the hard-won lessons now, they'll vanish under the weight of the next crisis, and you'll find yourself rebuilding from scratch instead of compounding forward.

Locking your lessons isn't about documentation. It's about defense, building a stronger foundation before the next storm. Here's how you lock the right pieces in place:

- **Codify Three Personal Shifts.** What behaviors did you sharpen, and refuse to unlearn? These aren't wish list items, they're non-negotiables that become part of how you lead from now on.

- **Codify Three System Shifts.** Which systems, rhythms, or norms changed for the better? Lock them in visibly, so the next wave of noise doesn't wash them away.

- **Capture One Big Cultural Story.** What story about your team, your leadership, or your culture changed because of this ascent? Frame it, tell it, and repeat it, because if you don't anchor a new story, the old one will quietly take its place again.

This isn't about admiring what you survived. It's about setting the stage to climb faster and higher the next time you launch.

Step 3: Prime the Next Ascent Loop—Build Smarter, Climb Higher, and Build Your Next 90-Day L.E.A.D. Laboratory

You're not patching together another loop. You're launching the next 90-Day L.E.A.D. Laboratory with new milestones, new goals, and new experiments. Momentum doesn't preserve itself. It must be reclaimed, re-aimed, and re-engineered. Otherwise, it dies quietly while you're still running. The leaders who climb fastest aren't the ones who coast after a win. They are the ones who use the heat from their last ascent to fuel the next one.

Remember the chain: Every experiment drives an objective, every objective supports a swimlane goal, and every swimlane goal pushes your quarterly milestone forward. This is how real progress is built. It has to be tight, focused, and aligned from experiment to vision.

Here's how to prime your next 90-Day Ascent Loop with intention, not inertia:

1. **Set the Milestone and Map the Chain.** Start with the next milestone. What does success look like 90 days from now, and has that target shifted based on the last cycle? Once it's clear, define what needs to shift in each swimlane to get there. From milestone to swimlane and goals to specific objectives, build the full alignment chain before you move.

2. **Design Smarter Experiments.** Now create experiments that match your refined objectives. Let your last 90 days inform this. What worked? What stalled? Design experiments that are smaller, sharper, and built to drive real signal fast.

3. **Tighten the Scoreboard.** Update your scoreboard to match the new game. Strip it down to the essentials, lead measures that actually drive momentum and show early movement. If it doesn't spark action, cut it.

4. **Reinforce One Leadership or Cultural Habit.** Choose one shift in behavior, mindset, or cultural tone that deserves intentional focus this cycle. Name it, track it, and build it into how you lead and how your team operates.

5. **Announce the Horizon.** Say where you're going next. Make the vision visible, even if it's only to yourself. Declare the milestone, the commitment, and the new edge you're leading from. Clarity creates energy, and your next ascent needs both.

You don't climb higher by luck. You climb because you build sharper loops, and you launch them before comfort slows you down.

Coach's Commentary

Strategic leaders don't wait to feel ready; they build what makes readiness irrelevant.

Driving Question

☞ Are you leading your next ascent, or just hoping momentum drags you along?

Remember, hope is not a leadership move. The next level doesn't come from coasting. It comes from conscious decisions to build, sharpen, and climb.

Your Coaching Question From Jim

☞ What's the one leadership move you must build, and the one you must bury, to climb higher in your next 90 days?

Write them down, declare them, and build the next 90 days around that spine, not around what feels easy.

Mini Challenge: Launch Your Next Ascent Loop

✍ Download Worksheet: W14 – Ascent Loop Launch Plan

Your Challenge:

- **Identify Two to Three High-Impact Plays.** One in Lean, one in Empower, and one in Amplify or Durability.

- **Anchor Your Flywheels.** Set your weekly 30-Day Flywheel loops:

  ○ Red / Yellow / Green scans

  ○ Scoreboard updates

  ○ One acceleration move

  ○ One adjustment move

- **Declare Your Evolution Theme.** This isn't a motto. It's your through-line. The identity shift you're chasing should shape your experiments, guide your leadership moves, and anchor your climb. Name it clearly. Carry it boldly. Examples:

  ○ *"Strategic Signal, Not Noise."*

  ○ *"Culture Builder, Not Bystander."*

  ○ *"Durable Under Pressure."*

- **Design Your Celebration Plan.** Mark the wins at 30, 60, and 90 days. Remember, no silent victories. Momentum multiplies when it's recognized.

- **Set Your First Checkpoint Now.** Book your 30-day flywheel review now, before life gets loud.

Reminder: This isn't about "working harder." It's about building the next stronger version of you, on purpose.

Final Reframe: Ascent Isn't Given. It's Engineered.

If you remember nothing else from this chapter, or from this entire Six-Step Leadership Challenge, remember this:

No one is coming to save your momentum. No one is handing you resilience. No one is granting you evolution. You build it and you earn it, one flywheel, one ascent loop, and one uncompromising move at a time.

The leaders who rise? They don't guess right. They outlearn. They out-adapt. They outlast everyone still waiting for the perfect moment. You want to lead like a CEO? Then stop waiting. Start building. Don't coast. Don't stall. Don't hope. Move, adjust, and fire the next loop. This isn't a tidy ending. This is ignition. You've got the system. You've got the rhythm. You've got the damn proof.

So, climb harder, smarter, and stronger than before. This is your lab, your loop, your ascent. Now go. Tighten it. Run it. Write the next chapter that makes this one look tame.

I'll see you at the next level.

CHAPTER 15

Make It Yours, Lock in the Operating System

Your leadership system isn't what you preach;
it's what you repeat.

– Jim Saliba

You didn't come this far for a few leadership hacks. You came to learn how to run your world differently, and you are. You've designed. You've iterated. You've flown the loop and felt the momentum. Now it's time to make it permanent.

This chapter isn't about reflection. It's about **normalization**. You are no longer running someone else's framework. You are running **your system**, the one that helps you see patterns faster, move with clarity, build trust on purpose, and evolve through real challenges. Step 6 of the Six-Step Leadership Challenge ends here, but the real work begins now because evolution isn't a moment. It's a method. And your method just became a **Personal Operating System**.

You're Not Running a Plan Anymore, You're Leading From Identity

Tools change outcomes. Systems change behavior. But identity? Identity changes everything.

You're no longer the person who *tries* to lead with clarity, consistency, and courage. You are someone who **does**. You don't need to wait for permission. You don't need to check the book. You don't need to psych yourself up.

This operating system, your Ascent Loop, your experiments, your flywheel rhythm, is who you are now. You don't use it once. You *run* it and you *live* it. Because here's the real shift:

You're not running a framework anymore. It's running you, in the best way.

This is what durable leadership looks like. Not flashy. Not frantic. Just **friction-proof, focus-driven**, and **fail-forward** by design.

YOUR PERSONAL LEADERSHIP OPERATING SYSTEM

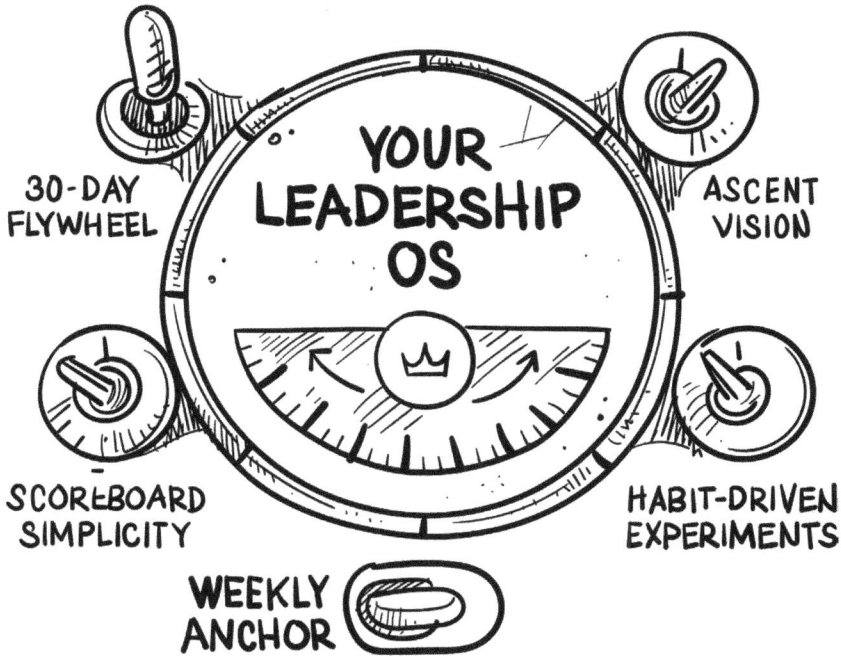

YOUR LEADERSHIP OS

30-DAY FLYWHEEL

ASCENT VISION

SCOREBOARD SIMPLICITY

HABIT-DRIVEN EXPERIMENTS

WEEKLY ANCHOR

Normalize the Rhythm, So It Becomes Real Life

Let's make this clear, for the readers *and* the listeners: You're not just running leadership tactics anymore. You're running a **Personal Leadership Operating System**, one that holds, flexes, and scales with you. Here's what that system looks like:

A Weekly Anchor Ritual

This is your *Cadence of Accountability*. One set time each week to reflect, recalibrate, and recommit. You don't wait for fires. You check in before they spark.

A Simple Scoreboard

Not a dashboard with fifty metrics. A real scoreboard your team can glance at and *instantly* know if they're winning. Simple. Visible. Actionable.

A 30-Day Flywheel

Every month, you run one tight loop:

- Red/Yellow/Green scan of your key moves
- One acceleration
- One adjustment
- One reflection
- One reset

No fluff. Just flywheel momentum that compounds.

Experiments, Not Endless Hustle

You're not muscling through. You're testing, tweaking, and learning. Every bold bet is a *sharpened experiment*, aimed at your next edge.

An Ascent Vision

You're not leading just to survive. You've got a future-facing identity guiding every loop. It's the leader you're becoming, declared, visible, and fueling the climb.

This isn't a checklist. It's a living system. It runs *with* you, even when energy dips and noise gets loud. You don't need to feel ready. You need to run the system. Not perfectly, but consistently. Because **repetition builds identity**, and **identity builds culture**.

You're not winging it anymore. You're running it.

At this point, you've built something many never do: a replicable system for leading when it matters most. But even the best systems collapse without a guiding north star. Let's name yours.

Bring Back Your Impact Ladder Check

You've spent the last chapters building your operating system. The flywheels, experiments, and rhythms you've created aren't just there to keep you busy. They're the tools that move you up the Impact Ladder.

Remember in earlier chapters, after each real story, we paused for a Ladder Check. We didn't do that in the system-build chapters, and that wasn't an accident.

Those chapters were about installing the practices that let you *move up the Ladder on purpose.*

You see, the Impact Ladder isn't just a description of your title. It's a diagnostic for how you lead, and you don't only move up. You can slide down, too. Pressure hits, stakes rise, reflexes kick in, and even seasoned leaders can drop from Architect back to Manager or from System Builder back to Bottleneck.

Your Operating System is how you catch that slide, course-correct, and keep climbing.

This is why you don't wait to "earn" Rung 5 or 6 to start practicing it. You install the rhythms now. You test the experiments now. You model the mindset now. Because leading at a higher rung isn't something you wait for. It's something you *practice.*

So, as you lock in your system, bring the Ladder Check back. Run it on yourself regularly. Ask yourself:

- What rung am I really operating from right now?

- What would moving one rung up look like over the next 30 days?

- What systems, habits, or experiments would support that shift?

Because the system you built here isn't just how you work. It's how you rise.

Build Your Personal Ascent Vision

If you've made it this far, you're not just running leadership moves anymore. You're building a personal operating system that scales with you. Now it's time to step back and name the bigger arc: Not just what you're doing, but who you're becoming.

Your Ascent Vision isn't a title or a promotion. It's the leader you are building through every flywheel, every cycle, every climb.

Earlier in this book, I mentioned one of my daughters and the running adventures we've taken on together. Well, my other daughter and I geeked out on something a little different, teaching. While she was still earning her degree, she started teaching intro psych at a local college. Around the same time, I had just finished my MBA and got invited to teach Information Systems.

We'd compare notes on everything from designing exams to grading chaos to the weird stuff students do when they think professors aren't paying attention. Later, she went on to become a certified life coach, makes sense, since her degree was in neuropsychology, and now we trade coaching insights like favorite podcasts. From trust-building to client-finding to how to survive marketing without losing your soul, those convos are some of my favorites.

Why does it matter here? Because leadership isn't about being perfect, it's about being in process. And the people who challenge your thinking and cheer you on while you're still figuring it out? That's part of the system too.

Ask yourself:

- What kind of leader do I want my next 90 days to *prove* I'm becoming?

- What habits, systems, and stories must become non-negotiable for me now?

- If my team could describe my leadership in one sentence, 90 days from today, what do I want them to say?

Clarity beats motivation, and vision beats willpower. When the noise hits, and it always does, it's not tactics that save you. It's the spine of who you're becoming. Anchor that vision now. Write it down. Let it shape the next ascent, and every ascent after that.

Your Ascent Vision isn't just a feel-good statement; it's the engine behind your leadership system, and here's how it powers your next move: At the center is your Vision, the identity of the leader you're becoming. Surrounding that are your Strategic Pillars, the focus areas that keep your leadership aligned and intentional. And on the outer ring: your 90-Day Experiments, the concrete actions that turn ideas into traction.

This is the full stack. Your vision drives your priorities. Your priorities drive your experiments. Your experiments build your reality. Want a reminder? Sketch this as three concentric circles. Put it on your wall, your whiteboard, or your team wiki. If they can see it, they'll help you build it.

Mini Challenge: Cement Your Personal Operating System

✍ Download Worksheet: W15 – Personal Ascent Blueprint

Your Challenge:

1. Capture Your Core Operating System

- Write down the three to five non-negotiable leadership habits you're taking forward. These aren't "good ideas." They're your new defaults.

2. Name Your Next Ascent Identity

- Complete the sentence: "In my next 90 days, I will lead like a _____." (Example: Strategic Architect, Culture Builder, or Visibility Multiplier.)

3. Lock Your Weekly Flywheel Rituals

- Red/Yellow/Green scan

- Scoreboard review

- One experiment acceleration

- One system adjustment

4. Create Your Ascent Reminder

- Design one simple anchor you'll see every week, a sticky note, a calendar reminder, a journal prompt, that keeps your Ascent Vision in front of you.

Reminder: You're not "starting over." You're compounding forward, on purpose.

Final Reframe: Leadership Isn't a Finish Line.

It's a flywheel. You build it, you run it, you become it.

If you remember nothing else from this chapter, remember this:

This isn't a finish line. It's a system you grow into, one ascent loop, one flywheel, one bold move at a time.

The leaders who stay sharp, stay durable, and stay dangerous (in the best way) aren't coasting on past wins. They're normalizing growth as a lifestyle. You don't need to wait for a promotion to lead like you're at the next level. You don't need to wait for a title change to start operating at a higher altitude. You have the system. You have the method. You have the flywheels already spinning. So now? Now it's just about building higher, every single cycle.

You are not standing still. You are ascending.

CHAPTER 16

Build the Future Only You Can See

Caretakers preserve. CEOs build.
You get to choose which future you're creating.

– Jim Saliba

This isn't your peak. It's your platform.

The Six-Step Leadership Challenge wasn't designed to end at the close of one 90-Day Ascent Loop. It was designed to launch you into the next level, and the level after that, and the level only *you* can build.

Leadership isn't a one-summit story. It's a relentless climb. It's about shaping a future that didn't exist until *you* stepped in to lead, build, and scale it. You're not running someone else's playbook anymore. You've built your own **leadership operating system**, and it works.

If you're serious about leadership, there is no "maintenance mode." No standing still. Only two directions: **Ascend or drift.**

This chapter is about making sure you keep ascending. Not by accident. Not by reaction. By **conscious, strategic, relentless design.** You've already built the lab, your L.E.A.D. system, flywheels, scoreboard, habits, and culture. Now it's time to **own it**. Turn it into a growth engine that compounds clarity, not just effort.

You're not a player waiting for the next move. **You're the architect.** And the future? It's waiting for you to **build it like you own the place.**

The Myth We're Breaking: "Once I'm successful enough, I'll finally get to slow down."

No. You won't.

This myth has killed more leaders' futures than any mistake they ever made on the way up. *The path forward isn't a straight line to comfort; it's a climb that keeps demanding more of you.* It's a series of climbs, each one steeper, smarter, and more deliberate than the last. The higher you go, the harder the choices, the bigger the responsibility, and the narrower the margin for drifting, doubting, or defaulting to comfort.

The future you're aiming for, the one only you can build, won't arrive through passive momentum. It will be created through **intentional ascent**.

The leaders who keep rising are the ones who understand:

- Success doesn't buy you rest.

- Growth doesn't mean you can coast.

- The next level demands a new version of you.

Now, let's be honest: You won't just climb in one direction forever. You'll slip or get pulled back a rung when the heat's on, but that's not failure. That's the signal to catch yourself, adjust, and climb again.

The leaders who stagnate, on the other hand, are the ones who start believing they've "arrived" and stop building. They get caught in the gravity of comfort and fall harder when the ground shifts.

The future doesn't show up on your calendar. You have to forge it. The good news is you've already got the tools, and you don't need the title before you start. Don't wait for someone to hand you Rung 5 or 6. Build the systems, shape the culture, and practice the altitude now, so when the opportunity comes, you're already there.

Remember the Impact Ladder? This isn't just about running loops for the sake of it. Every flywheel you build and every experiment you test is how you climb rungs. You're not just managing what is. You're architecting what could be.

How to Architect What Comes Next: Building the Future on Purpose

You're not guessing anymore. You're not wondering if you have what it takes. You've built the rhythms, earned the muscle, and proven you can adapt, ascend, and create systems that scale you, not just your output. Now it's time to design what comes next, on purpose.

This next phase isn't about trying harder. It's about leading with what works. You've run the Six-Step Leadership Challenge once. Now you own it. It's your turn to run the loop again, sharper and more intentionally. Here's how to build it from the inside out.

- **Introspection.** Keep scanning your signal. Your growth edge is still speaking.

- **Extrospection.** Tune your awareness wider. Lead up, across, and out, not just within.

- **Storyboard Your Future.** Keep casting your vision with clarity. Your team deserves a summit to climb toward.

- **Action Strategy.** Map your boldest moves. Not busyness, leverage.

- **Action Reaction.** Run tighter loops. Adjust faster. Shrink the distance between signal and shift.

- **Retrospect and Celebrate.** Don't skip the harvest. That's where the next loop finds its fuel.

You're not just using the system, you are the system now. Every new loop is yours to shape. This is your ascent, your system, your next level. Now, go architect what comes next because this time, you're not starting from scratch. You're starting from strength. Every time you run the loop, you're not just checking boxes. You're climbing. You're moving from Doer to Manager to Architect. From Bottleneck to System Builder. From reflex to design.

Final Reframe: Leadership Doesn't End. It Expands

If you remember nothing else from this final chapter, or from this book, let it be this:

You don't just run a system. You keep building it.

The Six-Step Leadership Challenge isn't something you finish. It's how you keep leading, building, and scaling your impact every quarter.

You don't lead because you have a title. You lead because you act like it's already yours.

You've proven you can do the work. Now prove you can keep climbing. Because intentional leaders don't close the book and stop. They take what they've built and go design the next chapter on purpose.

EPILOGUE

You're Already in Motion

Growth isn't about getting ready; it's about getting moving.
Your next ascent starts with what you do next.

– Jim Saliba

The Six-Step Leadership Challenge didn't hand you a ladder. It handed you the damn blueprints to build one. And this book, *Lead Like a CEO*, didn't give you a checklist. It gave you an operating system to live, lead, and scale on purpose. Not just once. Not just when it's easy. Every cycle and every climb. You didn't just learn a method. You built a leadership engine that runs because of you. You don't need more permission. You don't need a nicer title. You don't need to wait for someone else to say you're ready. You've got the system, you've got the flywheels, and you're already in motion, even if it doesn't always feel graceful.

The leaders who keep rising aren't waiting for perfect conditions. They're the ones who tune their systems, tighten their loops, and build the future before anyone else even sees it. So, here's the real question:

How high are you willing to climb?

Because the next level isn't waiting to welcome you. It's waiting for you to *build it*. One decision. One flywheel. One unglamorous, unsexy, unskippable day at a time.

Stay Connected

Leadership is a living system, and it's always evolving. If this book sparked something for you, let's keep building!
Website: www.jamessaliba.com

LinkedIn: linkedin.com/in/jamessaliba
Livestreams, articles, and new experiments: Follow for weekly leadership insights and tools.

If you're ready to take your ascent even further, I work with leaders who aren't just looking to climb higher, but are ready to *build* the mountain.

Wherever you are in your journey, remember: You don't lead because it's easy. You lead because you were built for more.

I'll see you at the next summit.

Leadership Resource Toolbox Recap

The Six-Step Leadership Challenge

Your leadership operating system

1. ***Introspection*** – *Know your story and strengths*

2. ***Extrospection*** – *Map the system and culture around you*

3. ***Storyboard Your Future*** – *Create a vivid vision*

4. ***Action Strategy*** – *Build your 90-day ascent plan*

5. ***Action + Reaction*** – *Run small experiments, adjust fast*

6. ***Retrospect + Celebrate*** – *Extract the lessons and evolve*

The L.E.A.D. Lab

Your 90-day playbook for action

- ***Lean into your story*** – *Clarity, mindset, and strategic identity*

- ***Empower your story*** – *Systems, delegation, ownership*

- ***Amplify your story*** – *Influence, trust, visibility*

- ***Durability for your story*** – *Brand, resilience, balance*

The Strategy Stack

Vision	What future are you building
	↓
Goals (Milestones)	What does success look like in 90 days?
	↓
Objectives	What outcomes move the system forward?
	↓
Experiments	What small, strategic test will you run?
	↓
Tasks	What actions will bring the experiment to life

The 30-Day Flywheel

Your momentum loop

Design → Act → Track → Reflect → Adapt

A tight, visible feedback loop that drives smarter motion.

The 90-Day Ascent Loop

Your leadership evolution cycle

Harvest Lessons → Lock the System Shift → Design the Next Ascent

*Don't just finish, **build stronger** with each cycle.*

R/Y/G Scan

Quick status tool for any experiment

- **Red** – *Kill it. Free up your focus.*

- **Yellow** – *Tune it. Friction = Feedback.*

- **Green** – *Accelerate it. Build on what's working.*
  Scoreboard vs. Dashboard

Only one drives action.

Scoreboard	Dashboard
Simple, visible	Complex, buried
Team-facing	Manager-facing
Lead indicators	Lag indicators
Motivates action	Tracks status
Updated weekly	Updated monthly

If it doesn't help people act, it doesn't belong on the scoreboard.

Leadership Experiment Library

We've tested over 50 real-world experiments that leaders use to build momentum, drive culture, and solve tough challenges across the L.E.A.D. swim lanes: Lean, Empower, Amplify, and Durability. These aren't ideas—they're field-tested actions used in our premium VIP intensives and the library continues to grow every month as more leaders run and refine them.

Want a taste? A few select experiments are included in the free Bonus Tools + Leadership Downloads. Here's a quick sample:

	Experiment Title	Description

Lean	Adaptive Horizons	Construct a future-back strategy from personal and market signals.
	Pattern Hunter	Build next-level self-awareness by tracking your behavioral loops.
	Balanced Scorecard	Build strategy alignment using a four-quadrant performance view.
Empower	Delegation Heat Map	Get clarity and courage on what to let go—and who owns what.
	Power Metric Mapping	Map key metrics that drive real influence and team focus.
	Strategic Decision Mapping	Design a team-ready playbook for better, faster decision-making.
Amplify	Cross-Functional Playbook	Create structure for influence when you lead across silos.
	Team SWOT to Triumph	Build awareness and alignment by mapping your team's strengths and gaps.
	Culture Compass	Shift your team from culture drift to culture by design.
Durability	Crisis Leadership: The Calm Inside the Storm	Step up as a steadying force when the pressure's on.
	Feedback Culture Builder	Create an environment where feedback flows freely—and usefully.
	Influence Without Authority	Lead change even when you don't have the title or control.

Coaching Prompts That Hit Hard

Use them in your own head or with your team

- *"What are we trying to learn with this?"*

- *"What does success actually look like?"*

- *"Where are we still asking for permission?"*

- *"What story are we reinforcing with this action?"*

- *"What small, bold move could shift this fast?"*

Let's Keep Going

You've just finished this book, but your leadership climb is just beginning. If you're ready to take the next step, here's how we can stay connected:

☑ Apply for 1-on-1 Coaching

Work with me directly to architect your next 90-day ascent. I take on a limited number of coaching clients, but if you're serious about leading at the next level, apply here:

☞ jamessaliba.com/coaching

☑ Get the Weekly Leadership Download

Join my email list for fresh experiments, livestream recaps, and tools you can use every week.

☞ jamessaliba.com/newsletter

☑ Unlock the Bonus Tools + Leadership Downloads

Grab printable worksheets, sample experiments, and extras to help you run your leadership system with even more clarity.

☞ jamessaliba.com/leadlikeaceobonus

☑ Share the Book With Your Team

Know someone who needs this message? A rising leader stuck in the weeds? A manager ready to level up? Share the book, or better yet, run a team experiment together.

The next step is yours.
You don't need a new job to lead at the next level.
You need a rhythm.
You need a challenge.
You need a system that sticks.

I'll see you on the next ascent,
Jim

✒ Bring This Message to Your Team or Event

Jim Saliba delivers keynote talks, executive sessions, and hands-on workshops on the very challenges this book unpacks, from building visible leadership to designing flywheels that drive culture, clarity, and results.

Whether you're hosting a conference, leading an internal leadership program, or building momentum with your executive team, Jim brings:

- 30 years of real-world leadership experience

- A sharp, no-fluff speaking style that cuts through the noise

- Practical playbooks and tools your audience can use immediately

Available formats:

- Keynote Talks

- Executive Workshops

- Leadership Offsite Sessions

- Virtual Masterclasses

- Train-the-Trainer Programs

Popular topics include:

- *Lead Like a CEO*

- *Stop Operating Two Levels Below Where You Should Be*

- *Designing a Leadership Flywheel That Actually Sticks*

- *The Six-Step Leadership Challenge*

To book Jim or inquire about availability:

speaking@jamessaliba.com

www.jamessaliba.com/speaking

About the Author

Jim Saliba is an executive coach, leadership strategist, and former vice president of a multi-billion-dollar tech company. Over three decades, Jim worked his way from software engineer to senior executive, leading teams, building systems, and navigating the chaos that comes with growth at scale. Along the way, he discovered that the biggest barriers weren't technical — they were leadership blind spots that left smart, capable people stuck two levels below their potential.

Today, Jim helps leaders close that gap. Through his coaching practice, he works with founders, directors, and senior executives who are ready to own their impact, lead with clarity, and stop getting dragged into the noise of day-to-day firefighting. He is the creator of the Six-Step Leadership Challenge, a practical framework for building momentum and scaling leadership without burning out.

Jim also hosts the Building Legendary Leaders podcast and livestream series, where he blends sharp strategy with the kind of grounded, real-world coaching leaders actually need. His work is known for being candid, practical, and sometimes just the right amount of kick-in-the-pants.

Based in San Jose, California, Jim splits his time between coaching, writing, and content creation. Away from work, you'll find him in the kitchen or the woodshop, crafting meals, handmade gifts, and conversations that matter.

Lead Like a CEO is his guidebook for leaders who don't want to wait for the perfect title to start showing up like it's already theirs.